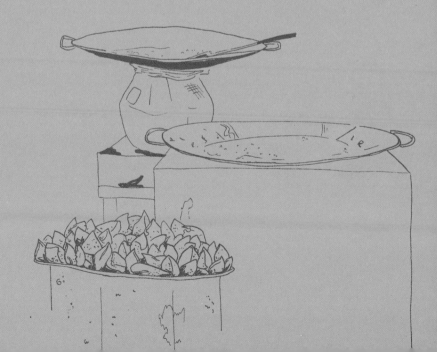

CHAI, CHAAT & CHUTNEY

CHAI, CHAAT & CHUTNEY

A STREET FOOD JOURNEY THROUGH INDIA

· · · · · · · · · · · · · · · · · ·

Chetna Makan

MITCHELL BEAZLEY

An Hachette UK Company
www.hachette.co.uk

First published in Great Britain in 2017 by Mitchell Beazley,
an imprint of Octopus Publishing Group Ltd, Carmelite
House, 50 Victoria Embankment, London EC4Y 0DZ
www.octopusbooks.co.uk
www.octopusbooksusa.com

Distributed in the US by Hachette Book Group,
1290 Avenue of the Americas, 4th and 5th Floors,
New York, NY 10104

Distributed in Canada by Canadian Manda Group,
664 Annette St., Toronto, Ontario, Canada M6S 2C8

ISBN 978-1-78472-287-6

A CIP catalogue record for this book is available
from the British Library.

Printed and bound in China.

10 9 8 7 6 5 4 3

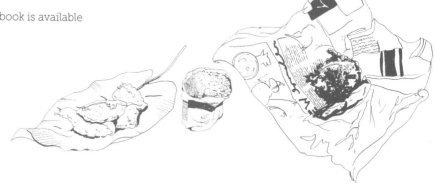

Commissioning Editor: Eleanor Maxfield
Art Director: Juliette Norsworthy
Senior Editor: Leanne Bryan
Photographers: Nassima Rothacker (studio)
  & Keith James (location)
Food Stylist: Lizzie Kamenetkzy
Props Stylist: Hannah Wilkinson
Illustrators: Amber Badger & Ella McLean
Production Manager: Caroline Alberti

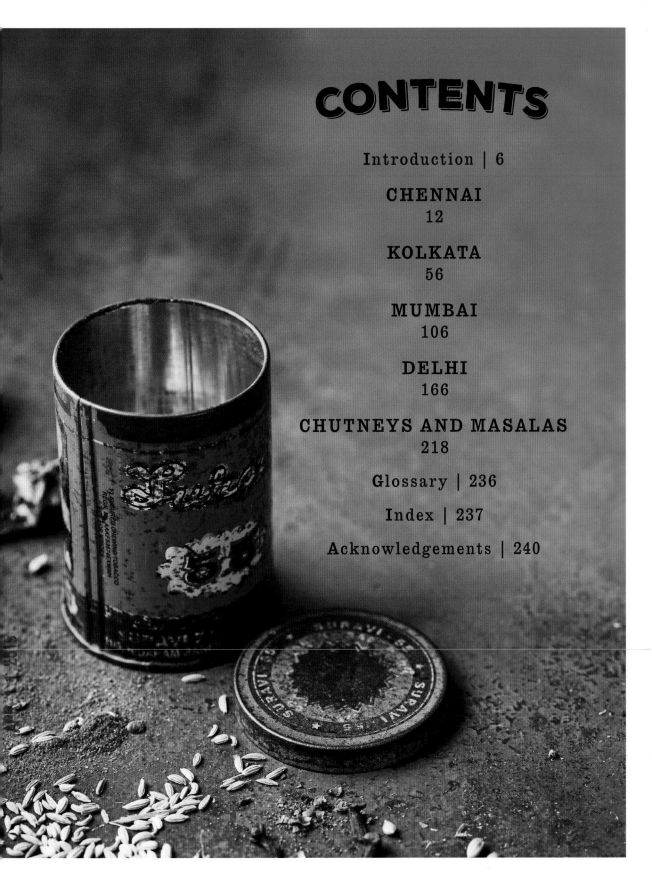

CONTENTS

Introduction | 6

CHENNAI
12

KOLKATA
56

MUMBAI
106

DELHI
166

CHUTNEYS AND MASALAS
218

Glossary | 236

Index | 237

Acknowledgements | 240

INTRODUCTION

Food is a big part of Indian life. Just as the weather is a common talking point in the **UK**, food is a popular subject of conversation in India. It is said that while Indians are eating breakfast, they are discussing what they will eat for lunch, and when eating lunch, dinner is the topic. This idea always makes me laugh, but it's mostly true!

Street food is a huge and important part of India's food culture. I love the fact that it is such a leveller – no matter what your background might be, standing at a popular street stall next to the other customers, you are all simply people enjoying the food. Some turn up in luxury cars, others on bicycles, but they're all there to experience the food made by that vendor.

Most street food is freshly prepared to order, served very quickly and, best of all, extremely cheap. Not only can you buy snacks and light dishes to keep you going, but you will also find on offer amazing meals, complete with a variety of flavours and components. And, yes – there are also sweets to enjoy!

Life has been an incredible journey for me from Jabalpur, the small town in central India where I grew up, hoping to go to fashion college one day. That dream came true when,

at 17 years of age, I went to study in Mumbai. I loved the whole process of creating – the concept that a simple thought passing through my mind could be developed as an idea and realized as a beautiful garment, but Mumbai was a big jump from the comforts of home.

At home, my mother cooked every day. She was always trying new things and encouraged me into the kitchen at a very young age. She would make birthday cakes for the family and slowly I joined in and eventually took over that role. It was nothing fancy – just simple sponge cakes made with love, but my friends and family enjoyed them.

At times, my family would go out for street food. Our favourites were the chaat (sour and spicy street food snacks) – bhel puri, pani puri and papdi chaat. The stall that made the best chaat in Jabalpur still exists! The next generation of

stallholders gradually learned the tricks of the trade, so whenever I visit my parents, I make sure to go there and enjoy some more of what I consider to be the best chaat I've ever tasted.

Another favourite type of street food my family loved to eat was South Indian food, especially the dosa (crispy south Indian crêpes made from fermented rice and lentil batter) and sambhar (south Indian stew made from lentils and tamarind). My dad would always have vada (fried snacks made from lentils, potatoes or vegetables) and sambhar, my sisters, plain dosa, and my mum and I would order masala dosa. To this day I remember what each of us ate, because every time we went out for this meal, we each had exactly the same thing!

Papa would also take us out for late night treats after he came home from work. He had a two-wheeled scooter and the three of us sisters would pile onto it and go to a special stall for cashew nut and raisin ice cream. Sadly, that place no longer exists, but the taste of its wonderful ice cream is still very fresh in my memory.

Food-wise, Mumbai was very different from Jabalpur. Our college canteen served an amazing breakfast of poha (flattened rice flakes) and masala chai (Indian tea brewed with spices), which I used to enjoy, but the rest of my daily meals tended to be street food. There was a stall just outside the college that served tea and coffee with lots of little snacks all day. That is how I got hooked on tea and biscuits and, to this day, that is what I have first thing every morning.

As I moved through college and shifted to working as a designer, I lived in many different parts of Mumbai, which gave me the opportunity to discover more incredible street food. I would visit markets to search out unique fabrics and accessories, and so found more great places to eat at the same time.

That's how I discovered Mumbai's best falooda (popular Indian dessert made with syrup, basil seeds, glass noodles, milk and ice cream) in a tiny shop in the Crawford Market. It sold nothing but falooda, and the flavours, of which there were many, included delights such as saffron, rose and mango. When I recently returned to the city I sought out this shop and realized once again just how wonderful their falooda is.

After many years in Mumbai I moved to Kent in the UK, which was once again a big change for me, especially when it came to food. Of the many things I missed about Indian cuisine, street food was top of the list. I did try to cook a few of those dishes in my early days in England, but found it tricky to get the right ingredients at the time. Fortunately, things have changed.

Of course, coming to Britain introduced me to a whole new world of baking. Slowly I found myself baking for friends and family and absolutely loved it. This led to my appearance on the TV show *The Great British Bake Off*, which gave me all the confidence I needed for my baking experiments. And that, in turn, led to my first book, *The Cardamom Trail*, which is full of amazing spices and other flavours that will transform familiar sweet and savoury bakes into showstoppers.

But when it came to writing this book, what I really wanted to share with all you food lovers out there was my early passion for India's street food. The subject is so vast I couldn't possibly cover it all in one book, so the question was where to start. Then it occurred to me that the four biggest cities in India broadly represent the four corners of the country, and the street food culture from each city offers distinctive, mouthwatering dishes.

For this book, I have chosen my favourite street food dishes – the food that has stood out for me on my travels. All of them have a memory or flavour that is special to me, but I've been careful to select recipes that are easily made in home kitchens. You should be able to find most of the ingredients locally, apart from a handful that are required for special dishes, which should be readily available online.

The key to cooking great street food is to prepare everything in advance. Get all the ingredients and other things you need together, do all the chopping and other prepping, have your chutneys ready then, finally, bring the dish together when you are ready to eat.

I do hope that you will give these recipes a go and enjoy them as much as I do. They represent my own take on a wonderful branch of Indian cuisine that has not only proved popular all over the world but also provides a daily lifeline for many Indians.

CHENNAI

There is so much colour in the clothes that people wear in Chennai. They still like traditional attire – men in lungis and women in sarees – and, wherever you look, there are ladies and girls with flowers in their hair.

Chennai is the city with the best filter coffee to pair with the best South Indian cuisine. It may be small compared to other capital cities, but it has a vibrant street food culture and its favourite dishes are loved throughout India. Indeed, dosa and vada sell in restaurants, cafés and street stalls all over the world.

The food in Chennai is subtle, balanced and delicious. The city doesn't have the number and variety of moveable street stalls that Kolkata, Mumbai and Delhi can offer – the snacks are sold mainly at small cafés and in busy markets, which on Sundays are packed with families who come to shop and enjoy the street food.

On the corners of quiet streets you can find stalls selling complete meals such as rice and curry on banana leaves, and filled dosa with sambhar. You can also find some very famous old mess halls in Chennai, run by generations of the same families, where the food is made fresh for every meal and also served on big banana leaves.

I love that the food in Chennai tends to use few ingredients and spices. However, cooks do take a lot of time to perfect the fermentation of idli and dosa batters, and their efforts are well worth it. And as a chutney maven, I have to admit that Chennai has some of the best chutneys in India. With so many wonderful flavours, you'll be surprised at how simple they are to make.

You can eat the dishes in this chapter at any time of day and in any season – I could easily live on dosa for breakfast, lunch and dinner!

ONION

SAMOSAS

Super crispy on the outside and with a soft, sweet and spicy
onion filling inside, these samosas are sold in Chennai on
carts both large and small, beautifully displayed as a samosa
mountain decorated with fresh chillies.

1 tablespoon sunflower oil, plus
   extra for deep-frying
4 onions, finely chopped
1 teaspoon salt
1/2 teaspoon chilli powder
1 small green chilli, finely chopped
12 sheets of filo pastry
1 egg, beaten
extra small green chillies, to
   decorate (optional)
Peanut Chutney (see page 225) or
   Coriander and Spinach Chutney
   (see page 228), to serve

Heat 1 tablespoon of oil in a saucepan set over medium heat. Add the onions and cook for about 5 minutes, until they begin to soften. Add the salt, chilli powder and green chilli, mix well and set aside to cool.

Take 1 sheet of pastry and cut it into strips, each 5cm (2 inches) wide. While you work with each piece, keep the other pastry sheets covered with a damp tea towel to prevent the pastry from drying out. Set 1 strip of pastry on your work surface and place a heaped tablespoon of the onion mixture at 1 end. Fold 1 corner of the pastry over the filling to form a triangle, then continue folding in alternate directions along the strip to make a triangular parcel. Brush the loose end with beaten egg and seal the triangle. Place the filled samosa on a plate and cover

the plate with a damp tea towel so the pastry doesn't dry out while you continue making samosas with the remaining pastry and onion mixture.

Fill a deep-fat fryer or a large saucepan with enough oil for deep-frying the samosas (ensuring the pan is no more than one-third full). Line a plate with some kitchen paper. Heat the oil to 190°C (375°F). Fry the samosas in batches for about 2 minutes each, until golden brown. Watch them carefully as they cook, since the filo pastry browns quickly. Remove with a slotted spoon and transfer the samosas to the paper-lined plate to drain excess oil. Decorate with extra small green chillis, if you wish, and serve hot with Peanut Chutney or Coriander and Spinach Chutney.

TAMARIND-STUFFED CHILLIES

Spicy and crispy on the outside, and with a lovely sour flavour within, these stuffed chillies hail from the streets of South India. I first had them in London, at the house of my friend Sudhakar, who is very keen on street food and remembers them from his hometown. They make a lovely party canapé or snack served with a cup of tea.

15 small fat green chillies
70g (2½oz) tamarind paste
1 teaspoon carom seeds
100g (3½oz) gram (chickpea) flour
½ teaspoon salt
up to 120ml (4fl oz) water
sunflower oil, for deep-frying
sea salt flakes

With a sharp, pointed knife, slit the chillies lengthways along 1 side and remove the seeds and membranes.

Combine the tamarind paste and carom seeds in a small bowl and use this mixture to stuff each chilli. Set aside.

In another bowl, mix the gram flour and salt, then slowly add just enough of the measured water to make a runny batter.

Heat enough oil for deep-frying chillies in a deep-fat fryer or large saucepan (ensuring the pan is no more than one-third full) to 180°C (350°F). Line a couple of plates with some kitchen paper. Working in batches, dip each chilli in the batter, then carefully drop it into the hot oil and fry for about 2 minutes, until lightly coloured. Remove with a slotted spoon and transfer the chillies to a paper-lined plate to drain excess oil.

Once all the chillies have been fried, dip them once again into the batter and (again, working in batches), fry them a second time for 2 minutes, until golden brown and crispy. Transfer to a paper-lined plate to drain excess oil. Season with sea salt flakes and serve hot.

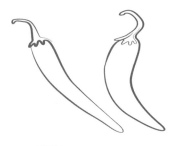

CHILLI PANEER

This yummy recipe is not only simple, it goes well with
a lot of other dishes, such as dal and rice, **Soft Kachori**
(*see* page 62) or, indeed, any flatbread in this book. It makes
a fabulous filling for **Plain Dosa** (*see* page 26), too.
You can also serve it as a party nibble – just offer cocktail
sticks alongside to help your guests pick it up, as you
would for marinated olives.

For the paneer
50g (1¾oz) plain flour
¼ teaspoon salt
6 tablespoons water
2 tablespoons sunflower oil
300g (10½oz) paneer, cut into
    flat slices

For the sauce
1 tablespoon sunflower oil
1 large onion, thinly sliced
2 small green chillies, finely
    chopped
1 tablespoon soy sauce
1 tablespoon chilli sauce
1 tablespoon ketchup
½ teaspoon salt
¼ teaspoon ground black pepper

To prepare the paneer, put the flour and salt into a bowl and gradually stir in the measured water to make a smooth batter.

Heat the oil in a frying pan over medium heat. Line a plate with some kitchen paper. Dip the cheese pieces in the batter, transfer them to the pan and fry for about 1 minute on each side, until golden brown. Remove the cooked paneer pieces with a slotted spoon and transfer to the paper-lined plate to drain excess oil.

To make the sauce, add the sunflower oil to the same frying pan in which you cooked the paneer and heat over medium heat. Add the onion and green chillies and fry for about 5 minutes, until the onion is light golden. Add the soy sauce, chilli sauce, ketchup, salt and pepper and mix well.

Transfer the battered paneer to the frying pan, mix the pieces into the sauce well, then take the pan off the heat, transfer the mixture to a serving bowl and serve hot.

CORN CHAAT

I found many people on the streets of Chennai and Mumbai enjoying this simple snack. In Chennai the vendors were steaming the corn first, whereas in Mumbai, it was boiled. Although there aren't many ingredients, the flavours are perfectly balanced. Sweetcorn goes very well with the sourness of Chaat Masala, and the lime and coriander give this snack a beautiful finish.

500g (1lb 2oz) frozen sweetcorn kernels
1 tablespoon salted butter
½ teaspoon salt
½ teaspoon Chaat Masala (see page 230)
½ teaspoon chilli powder, plus extra to garnish (optional)
handful of fresh coriander leaves, finely chopped
1 tablespoon lime juice

Boil the sweetcorn in a saucepan for 10 minutes, then drain and set aside.

Melt the butter in a wide saucepan set over medium heat and add the salt, Chaat Masala and chilli powder. Tip in the drained sweetcorn and mix well. Take the pan off the heat.

Add the coriander and lime juice and give the mixture another good stir. Garnish with extra chilli powder, if liked, and serve warm or cold.

PLAIN

DOSA

My mum makes amazing dosa meals and I learned how to make them from her. Plain dosa is traditionally eaten with Sambhar and Coconut Chutney, but it can also be stuffed with fillings such as the potato one opposite. You'll need to begin making the batter a couple of days in advance of cooking. *See* photograph, pages 28–29.

300g (10½oz) white rice
900ml (1½ pints) water
100g (3½oz) split black lentils
  (urad dal)
10g (¼oz) fenugreek seeds
sunflower oil, for frying

To serve
Sambhar (*see* page 33)
Coconut Chutney (*see* page 221)
Coriander and Spinach Chutney
  (*see* page 228)

Soak the rice overnight in 500ml (18fl oz) of the measured water. At the same time, in a separate bowl, soak the lentils and fenugreek seeds together in the remaining 400ml (14fl oz) measured water.

The next day, drain the rice and transfer it to a blender. Blend to a paste, adding a little water if necessary – be careful not to add too much as you want a thick paste. Repeat the process with the lentil and fenugreek mixture. Combine the 2 pastes in a bowl, cover with clingfilm and leave the mixture in a warm part of the kitchen for 24 hours to ferment. You will find that the batter rises a little and smells sour. At that point, transfer it to the refrigerator until you a re ready to cook.

Check the batter is the right consistency: it should be easy to spread, so blend in water accordingly. Heat a frying pan over high heat and add a few drops of oil. Once the pan is hot, wipe it carefully with kitchen paper so that it is greased, but dry. Pour a ladleful of batter into the frying pan and use the underside of the ladle bowl to spread the batter across the base of the pan into a large, thin dosa. Drizzle 1 teaspoon oil around the edges of the dosa and cook for 2–3 minutes, until golden (note that the dosa is cooked on only 1 side). Fold the dosa in half and transfer it to a plate. Repeat with the remaining batter.

Serve the dosa hot with Sambhar and the chutneys.

MASALA DOSA
FILLING

Although this delicious mixture is usually found stuffed inside a dosa, it can also be served on the side which, along with **S**ambhar and chutneys, makes a complete meal. If preferred, however, you could enjoy it as a sabji (vegetable dish) alongside bread or roti. When pre-cooking the potatoes, I like to keep the skins on so they don't disintegrate when boiled. *See* photograph, pages 28–29.

1 tablespoon sunflower oil
1 teaspoon mustard seeds
6 curry leaves
2 dried red chillies
1 tablespoon split chickpeas
   (chana dal)
1 teaspoon split black lentils
   (urad dal)
1 onion, roughly chopped
1½ teaspoons salt
½ teaspoon ground turmeric
4 floury potatoes, boiled, peeled
   and cut into small dice

Heat the oil in a wide saucepan over medium heat. Add the mustard seeds, curry leaves and dried chillies and, when they begin to sizzle, add the split chickpeas and lentils and cook, stirring, for 2 minutes.

Add the onion and cook for about 3–4 minutes, until it begins to colour. Stir in the salt and turmeric, then add the diced potatoes and mix well. Cook for a further 5 minutes, then remove the pan from the heat. Serve hot.

If you are serving this dish with Plain Dosa (*see* opposite), cook 8 dosa as directed, divide the potato filling into 8 portions, fill each dosa with 1 portion and fold in half to serve.

ONION AND TOMATO
UTTAPAM

Uttapam are much thicker than dosa, which is why it takes
a little longer to cook them. The result is not as crispy
as a dosa, but is totally delicious. Served with Sambhar and
chutneys, they are found all over India, in restaurants
as well as street stalls. You can make uttapam with all sorts
of toppings, but this onion and tomato combination
is my favourite.

1 onion, finely chopped
1 tomato, finely chopped
1 green chilli, finely chopped
1/2 teaspoon salt
4 ladlefuls of Plain Dosa batter
(*see* page 26)
sunflower oil, for frying

To serve
Sambhar (*see* page 33)
Coconut Chutney (*see* page 221)
Coriander and Spinach Chutney
(*see* page 228)

Put the onion, tomato, chilli
and salt into a bowl and give
them a good mix.

Heat a frying pan over
medium-low heat. When the
pan is hot, pour in a ladleful
of the dosa batter. Sprinkle
a quarter of the vegetable
mixture on top and spread
out the mixture to make a
10–13cm (4–5 inch) circle.
Drizzle a little oil around the
edges of the uttapam and
cook for 5 minutes on each
side. Remove the uttapam
from the pan and repeat with
the remaining ingredients to
make 3 more.

Serve the uttapam hot
with Sambhar, Coconut
Chutney and Coriander
and Spinach Chutney.

SAMBHAR

This South Indian-style lentil dish, one of the staples of
Chennai, can be served with dosa, idli, vada, rice and many
other dishes. It goes well with **Plain Dosa** (*see* page 26) or
Lemon Rice (*see* page 52). There are many ways to make it:
some people add vegetables such as carrots or drumsticks
(the long, slender, green seed pods of the *Moringa oleifera* tree,
regularly used in Indian cuisine); whereas others like it very
runny. These days you can find ready-made packs of sambhar
masala in shops, but I provide a recipe for this useful spice
blend on page 232. I like to make up a fresh batch as soon
as it runs out, so it's on hand whenever I need it.

250g (9oz) split pigeon peas
  (toor dal)
1 tablespoon split chickpeas
  (chana dal)
1 1/2 teaspoons salt
1 teaspoon ground turmeric
1.2 litres (2 pints) water
1 tablespoon sunflower oil
1 teaspoon mustard seeds
10 curry leaves
4 dried red chillies
1 onion, thinly sliced
2 tablespoons Sambhar Masala
  (*see* page 232)
1 tablespoon tamarind paste

Put both types of dal into a large pan with the salt, turmeric and measured water. Simmer for 30–35 minutes, or until tender.

In a separate large saucepan, heat the oil over medium heat and add the mustard seeds, curry leaves and dried chillies. Once they begin to sizzle, add the sliced onion and cook for about 5 minutes, until it begins to soften. Add the Sambhar Masala and mix well.

Tip the cooked dals into the onion mixture, then stir in the tamarind paste. (If the dals are too thick, add 100ml/3 1/2fl oz boiling water.) Mix well and cook for a final 5 minutes. Serve immediately.

MEDU VADA

These vada are super soft on the inside and crispy on the outside. They are so irresistible served soaked in Coconut Chutney and Sambhar, it's hardly a surprise that they have spread from the streets of Chennai to become a familiar sight in South Indian cafés and restaurants all over the world.

300g (10½oz) split black lentils (urad dal)
700ml (1¼ pints) water
1 small green chilli, chopped
2.5cm (1 inch) piece of fresh root ginger, peeled and chopped
10 curry leaves
¾ teaspoon salt
sunflower oil, for deep-frying

To serve
Coconut Chutney (*see* page 221)
Sambhar (optional; *see* page 33)

Soak the lentils in the measured water overnight. The next day, drain and put them into a blender or food processor with the green chilli, ginger, curry leaves and salt. Blend to a smooth paste. Add a little water, if necessary, to achieve the correct consistency, but add as little as possible as the batter needs to be thick.

Tip the batter into a bowl and beat it with a wooden spoon for 6–8 minutes to lighten the vada mixture. Pour enough oil into a deep-fat fryer or large saucepan to deep-fry the vada (ensuring the pan is no more than one-third full) and heat it to 170–180°C (340–350°F). Line a plate with kitchen paper.

To make the traditional vada shape with a hole in the centre, take a glass and place a sheet of flexible plastic (cut from a thick food bag) over the rim.

Hold the overhanging plastic against the sides of the glass to ensure the top of the glass remains covered. Wet the palm of your hand and run it over the plastic stretched over the top of the glass. Spoon 1½ tablespoons of the vada batter onto the plastic stretched across the top of the glass, pat it down to make a disc shape and poke a hole into the centre using your finger. Slide the vada gently off the plastic into the hot oil. Repeat until all the batter is used. (If you find this too tricky and time-consuming, simply pop spoonfuls of the batter directly into the hot oil.) Fry the vada in batches for 2–3 minutes, until golden. Remove with a slotted spoon and transfer to the paper-lined plate to drain excess oil while you fry the rest. Serve hot with Coconut Chutney, and Sambhar, if liked.

CAULIFLOWER PAKORA

These super-crispy, indulgent pakora are a must-try
with Tomato Chutney or Peanut Chutney. They are crispier
than regular pakora due to a double-frying process.
People don't generally associate cauliflower with pakora,
but different versions of these snacks are very popular
in North India and Chennai.

60g (2¹/₂oz) gram (chickpea) flour
1 green chilli, finely chopped
1 tablespoon toasted fennel seeds
¹/₂ teaspoon mango powder
   (amchur)
¹/₂ teaspoon salt
90–100ml (3–3¹/₂fl oz) water
sunflower oil, for deep-frying
1 medium cauliflower, cut into
   equal florets
Tomato Chutney (see page 225),
   Peanut Chutney (see page
   225) or Tamarind Chutney
   (see page 220), to serve

Combine the flour, chilli, fennel seeds, mango powder and salt in a bowl and mix well. Gradually mix in the measured water, stirring to make a batter that's runny enough to coat the back of the spoon.

Heat enough oil for deep-frying the pakora in a deep-fat fryer or large saucepan (ensuring the pan is no more than one-third full) to 180°C (350°F). Line a plate with some kitchen paper. Dip the cauliflower florets into the batter 1 at a time and carefully drop them into the hot oil (cook them in batches to avoid overcrowding the pan). Cook for 3–4 minutes, until the pakora begin to change colour. Drain with a slotted spoon and transfer the pakora to the paper-lined plate to drain excess oil.

Once you have fried the whole lot, take 1 pakora at a time and press it between your palms between 2 sheets of kitchen paper to flatten it. Take care not to press too hard – you don't want to squash it completely.

Increase the heat under the oil to bring the temperature of the oil to 190°C (375°F). Add the flattened pakora and fry (once again, in batches) for 2 minutes, until golden brown. Remove with a slotted spoon and transfer the pakora to a paper-lined plate to drain excess oil.

Serve hot with Tomato Chutney, Peanut Chutney or Tamarind Chutney.

MOONG DAL VADA

These vada are available in all shapes and sizes all over India. You can find them sold on huge street stalls as well as tiny operations run from a bicycle! They are best enjoyed piping hot in the monsoon season, when the cold weather makes hot fried foods a very welcome comfort. Enjoy them with a green chutney of your choice, such as **Coriander and Spinach Chutney** (*see* page 228), **Mint Chutney** (*see* page 228) or **Curry Leaf Chutney** (*see* page 229).

250g (9oz) yellow split lentils (moong dal)
2.5cm (1 inch) piece of fresh root ginger, peeled and finely chopped
1 green chilli, finely chopped
1 teaspoon salt
½ teaspoon black pepper
1 onion, finely chopped
handful of fresh coriander leaves, finely chopped
sunflower oil, for deep-frying
green chutney of your choice, to serve

Soak the lentils in twice their volume of cold water for 1 hour.

Drain the lentils, then put them into a blender with the ginger, chilli, salt and pepper and blend to a smooth paste. Add a couple of tablespoons of water, if needed, to loosen the mixture. Transfer the mixture to a bowl and whisk for 5 minutes until it is completely smooth.

Tip the paste into a bowl and stir in the onion and coriander until they are evenly distributed in the batter.

Heat enough oil for deep-frying the vada in a deep-fat fryer or large saucepan (ensuring the pan is no more than one-third full) over medium heat to 180°C (350°F). Line a plate with some kitchen paper. Once the oil is hot, use a tablespoon to carefully drop balls of the lentil mixture into the oil (cook them in batches to avoid overcrowding the pan). Fry the vada for roughly 2 minutes on each side, until golden and crisp. Drain with a slotted spoon and transfer the vada to the paper-lined plate to drain excess oil. Serve immediately, with green chutney.

RICE AND DAL PAPDI

These super-crispy snacks are available all over India from little street-side shops and stalls. I found the ones readily available in Chennai to be the tastiest, and this recipe is my take on that version. Enjoy them with any of the chutneys in this book plus a cup of Masala Chai (*see* page 217).

60g (2¼oz) split chickpeas
(chana dal)
125g (4½oz) rice flour
125g (4½oz) plain flour
1 teaspoon salt, plus extra
to garnish
½ teaspoon chilli powder
10 curry leaves, finely chopped
about 120ml (4fl oz) water
sunflower oil, for deep-frying
sea salt flakes
chutney of your choice, to serve
(optional)

Put the split chickpeas into a bowl, cover with water and leave to soak for 1 hour. Drain the split chickpeas, then grind them to a rough paste using a food processor, adding 1 tablespoon of water if necessary to achieve a rough, thick paste that isn't too runny.

Put the ground chickpeas, the rice four, plain flour, salt, chilli powder and curry leaves into a large bowl and mix well. Very gradually mix in just enough of the measured water (or a little more, if necessary), a few drops at a time, to bring the mixture together into a soft dough. Cover the bowl with clingfilm and leave to rest for 30 minutes.

Fill a deep-fat fryer or large saucepan with enough sunflower oil to deep-fry the papdi (ensuring the pan is no more than one-third full) and heat it to 190°C (375°F). Line a plate with some kitchen paper.

Take small portions of the dough, roughly the size of a grape, and roll them into thin discs with a diameter of 5cm (2 inches). Working in batches, fry the papdi for 2–3 minutes, until golden brown. Remove with a slotted spoon and transfer the papdi to the paper-lined plate to drain excess oil while you fry the remaining dough. Leave to cool, then season with sea salt flakes and serve with the chutney of your choice, if liked.

UPMA

This light and healthy South Indian dish was made
for breakfast every single day in my college canteen.
It takes minutes to prepare and tastes fresh and delicious.
Try it with Coconut or Peanut Chutney.

250g (9oz) semolina
1½ tablespoons sunflower oil
1 teaspoon black mustard seeds
pinch of asafoetida
8 curry leaves
2 tablespoons peanuts
10 cashew nuts
1 tablespoon split chickpeas
  (chana dal)
1.5cm (½ inch) piece of fresh
  root ginger, peeled and
  finely chopped
1 small green chilli, finely chopped
1 onion, finely chopped
1 carrot, finely chopped
1 green pepper, finely chopped
1½ teaspoons salt
850ml (1½ pints) boiling water
Coconut Chutney (see page 221) or
  Peanut Chutney (see page 225),
  to serve

Heat a dry frying pan, add the semolina and toast over low heat for 2 minutes, stirring constantly. Ensure the colour of the semolina does not change. Transfer to a bowl and set aside.

Heat the oil in a large saucepan over medium heat. Add the mustard seeds, followed by the asafoetida. Cook until the mixture sizzles, then add the curry leaves, peanuts, cashews and split chickpeas and cook over low heat for 2 minutes, until the ingredients begin to turn golden. Stir in the ginger and chilli and cook for 1 minute.

Add the onion, carrot, green pepper and salt to the saucepan. Carefully pour in the measured boiling water and simmer for 3–4 minutes, until the onion and peppers have softened slightly.

Very slowly add the toasted semolina to the saucepan, stirring continuously to prevent clumping. Cook for 3–4 minutes until all the water has been absorbed. Serve immediately with the chutney.

CHANA DAL
VADA

I found many variations of this **South Indian vada** in **Chennai** and also some in **Kolkata**. It's a very straightforward recipe, with only a little soaking for advance preparation, and goes extremely well with **Coconut Chutney** (*see* page 221) or **Curry Leaf Chutney** (*see* page 229). *See* photograph, page 45.

200g (7oz) split chickpeas (chana dal)
600ml (20fl oz) plus 1 tablespoon cold water
1 onion, finely chopped
1 garlic clove, finely chopped
1cm (1/2 inch) piece of fresh root ginger, peeled and finely chopped
1 small green chilli, finely chopped
5 curry leaves, roughly chopped
handful of fresh coriander leaves, finely chopped
1/2 teaspoon salt
1/2 teaspoon chilli powder
1/2 teaspoon ground cumin
sunflower oil, for deep-frying
chutney of your choice, to serve

Soak the split chickpeas in 600ml (20fl oz) of the measured water overnight or for at least 4 hours.

Drain the split chickpeas and tip them into a food processor or blender. Add the remaining 1 tablespoon measured water and grind them to a paste. Add the remaining ingredients, except the oil, and mix well to combine.

Heat enough oil for deep-frying the vada in a deep-fat fryer or large saucepan (ensuring the pan is no more than one-third full) to 180°C (350°F). Line a plate with some kitchen paper. Take a heaped tablespoon of the mixture in the palm of your hand and pat it into a disc shape. Pop it carefully into the hot oil and repeat with the remaining mixture to make 11 more (cook the vada in batches to avoid overcrowding the pan). Cook for 2 minutes, then turn the vada and cook for a further 2 minutes, or until golden brown. Remove with a slotted spoon and transfer the vada to the paper-lined plate to drain excess oil. Serve the vada hot, with chutney.

COCONUT
BOLI

Coconut boli, a scrumptiously sweet stuffed paratha, hails
from the South of India. In Mumbai, there is a variation
that is filled with sweet lentils called puran poli. My version
takes a little from each tradition. It is not particularly sweet,
but the combination of flavours is lovely.

For the dough
100g (10½oz) chapatti flour
100g (10½oz) plain flour
½ teaspoon ground turmeric
about 120ml (4fl oz) water

For the filling
150g (5½oz) split chickpeas
   (chana dal)
500ml (18fl oz) water
1 tablespoon ghee, plus extra
   for frying
100g (10½oz) freshly grated
   coconut
100g (10½oz) jaggery
1 teaspoon ground cardamom

To make the dough, put the flours and turmeric into a bowl and slowly mix in just enough of the measured water (or a little more, if necessary) to form a soft dough. Knead it for 2 minutes, then cover the bowl with clingfilm and leave to rest for 30 minutes.

To make the filling, put the split chickpeas into a saucepan with the measured water and bring to a boil. Reduce the heat to low and cook for about 35–40 minutes, until the chickpeas are soft and mushy.

In another pan, heat the ghee over medium to low heat, then add the coconut and cook for 1 minute. Add the jaggery and allow it to melt, then stir in the cooked chickpeas and cardamom powder. Mix well, then cook for 2–5 minutes,

using a potato masher to squash any lumps in the mixture. Set aside to cool.

Divide the dough into 12 small portions. Roll out 1 portion into a thin circle that measures 12–15cm (4½–6 inches) in diameter, then roll out another portion to the same size. Put 3–4 tablespoons of the coconut filling on 1 of the dough circles and spread it across the surface evenly. Lay the other circle on top and press around the edges to seal it well. Repeat with the remaining dough and filling to make 6 boli.

Heat a frying pan over medium heat. Cook each boli for 2–3 minutes on each side, until golden, adding ½ teaspoon of ghee to the pan as each side cooks. Serve hot.

CORNFLAKE
CHAAT

This dish is best enjoyed sitting on the seafront in Chennai, where the light, crunchy snack is sold in small paper cones. It's usually served dry but I sometimes use Tomato Chutney (*see* page 225) or Mint Chutney (*see* page 228) to give the flavours a little kick.

1 teaspoon sunflower oil
50g (1³/₄oz) peanuts
50g (1³/₄oz) plain cornflakes
50g (1³/₄oz) gram flour noodles
   (sev) or Bombay mix
¼ teaspoon salt
¼ teaspoon chilli powder
¼ teaspoon Chaat Masala
   (*see* page 230)
½ onion, finely chopped
juice of 1 lime

Heat the oil in a wide saucepan over medium heat. Line a plate with some kitchen paper. Add the peanuts to the hot oil and cook, stirring, for about 2 minutes, until golden brown. Transfer to the paper-lined plate to drain excess oil and leave to cool.

Combine the remaining ingredients in a large bowl and add the cooled fried peanuts. Mix well and serve immediately.

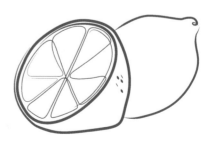

LEMON RICE

Lemon rice is very light and fresh. Enjoy it as part of a thali (a large Indian platter, made up of a selection of various dishes), on its own, or (my preference) with Sambhar or chutney – in Chennai I ate it with coconut chutney. The dish is so quick and simple to make, it's ideal for a speedy supper.

1 tablespoon sunflower oil
1½ teaspoons black mustard seeds
1½ teaspoons split black lentils
(urad dal)
1½ teaspoons split chickpeas
(chana dal)
4 dried red chillies
1 teaspoon salt
1 teaspoon ground turmeric
400g (14oz) white basmati rice
1 litre (1¾ pints) boiling water
3 tablespoons lemon juice

To serve (optional)
Sambhar (*see* page 33)
Coconut Chutney (*see* page 221) or
Coriander and Spinach Chutney
(*see* page 228)

Heat the oil in a wide saucepan. Add the mustard seeds, lentils, split chickpeas and dried chillies and cook over medium heat for about 1 minute, until they begin to sizzle. Stir in the salt and turmeric, then add the rice and mix well.

Slowly stir in the measured boiling water. Cover the pan with a lid and cook over low heat for 12 minutes, until the rice is cooked. Stir in the lemon juice. Serve hot with Sambhar and Coconut Chutney or Coriander and Spinach Chutney, if liked.

SWEET PONGAL

This dessert is traditionally served as part of the meal in South India, particularly during festivals, but it's also found in the street food thalis of Chennai. The lovely flavours of rice and lentils mixed with jaggery and dried fruit may seem unusual, yet the combination is thoroughly delicious.

100g (3¹/₂oz) long-grain rice
50g (1³/₄oz) split yellow lentils (moong dal)
900ml (30fl oz) water
2 tablespoons ghee
40g (1¹/₂oz) cashew nuts
40g (1¹/₂oz) raisins
100g (3¹/₂oz) jaggery
¹/₂ teaspoon ground cardamom

Put the rice, lentils and 800ml (1¹/₂ pints) of the measured water into a saucepan and leave to soak for 30 minutes. The lentils and rice will absorb most of the water during this time. Bring the rice and lentils to a boil and simmer over low heat for 30–35 minutes, until both are very tender. Then roughly mash them together in the saucepan with a potato masher until well combined.

Heat the ghee in a small saucepan set over medium heat and add the cashews and raisins. Cook for a couple of minutes, until they start to take on some colour. Tip them into the rice and lentil mixture and stir well.

Return the same small saucepan to the heat and add the jaggery with the remaining 100ml (3¹/₂fl oz) water and simmer until the jaggery has melted. Pass the caramel liquid through a sieve into the rice and lentil mixture. Add the cardamom and mix well. Transfer the saucepan to the hob and cook over medium heat for 5 minutes, until everything is evenly combined. Serve warm.

KOLKATA

Kolkata makes me want to travel back in time. It would be amazing to see how this city, with its beautiful architecture, worked in the past. The characterful, colourful old buildings still stand strong in the heart of the city, in the midst of all the traffic and chaos.

Kolkata is one vibrant city, unlike any other I've ever visited, and the street food has a soul of its own. While pav bhaji (spicy vegetable curry served with a soft buttered bread roll), samosa and kachori (small, crispy, pocket-shaped snacks) have become famous all over the country, the majority of street food here remains true to its Bengali origins, and that is what I love about this city. They are so proud of their food – and they should be, because it's truly incredible!

I have eaten everything, from snacks to full meals, on the streets of Kolkata, and I love the hustle and bustle of lunchtimes, as everyone eagerly rushes to their favourite stalls. You find all sorts of people enjoying the food.

A wide variety of thalis are sold on the streets. Fish is the highlight of most thalis, but they also include simple potato dishes, lentils and chops to provide delicious complete meals, many of which are served on plates made from leaves.

Kolkata is famous for its chaat, mouthwatering puchkas (crisp, puffed puri filled with spiced potato and spicy-sour liquid – also known as pani puri) and jhal muri (spiced puffed rice), all of which make lovely light snacks. The cuisine also features many varieties of lentils – in vada, chillas, dal with rice and more.

Add to the mix the beautiful architecture, colourful clothing, and the ladies' red and white bangles (shakha pola) and you'll find that, amidst the madness and chaos, it is very easy to fall in love with Kolkata.

POTATO, PANEER AND CHICKPEA CURRY

Soft, fluffy potato and cubes of paneer soak up the flavours of the sauce in this light, delicious curry, while the chickpeas add a lovely texture. This dish is very popular in **Kolkata** and best teamed with **Soft Kachori**, but if you want a healthier version, serve it with rice or chapattis.

2 tablespoons sunflower oil
2 onions, roughly chopped
4 tomatoes, roughly chopped
1 small green chilli, chopped
2 garlic cloves, chopped
2.5cm (1 inch) piece of fresh root
　ginger, peeled and chopped
200ml (1/3 pint) water
1 cinnamon stick
11/2 teaspoons salt
1 teaspoon granulated sugar
2 teaspoons garam masala
1/2 teaspoon ground turmeric
1/2 teaspoon chilli powder
100g (31/2oz) paneer, cubed
2 floury potatoes, boiled, peeled
　and cubed
400g (14oz) can chickpeas
Soft Kachori (see page 62),
　rice or chapattis, to serve

Heat 1 tablespoon of the oil in a saucepan over medium heat. Add the onions, tomatoes, chilli, garlic and ginger and cook for 10 minutes, or until everything is softened.

Transfer the mixture to a blender or food processor, add 100ml (31/2fl oz) of the measured water and blend to a smooth paste.

Heat the remaining oil in a saucepan over medium heat. Add the cinnamon stick and cook for a few seconds, then stir in the onion and tomato paste. Cover the pan with a lid and cook over low heat for 10–15 minutes, until well cooked.

Add the salt, sugar, spices and the remaining 100ml (31/2fl oz) measured water to the pan and mix well. Stir in the paneer, potatoes and the chickpeas along with their canning liquid. Cover and cook for about 10 minutes, until the sauce thickens and the potatoes are tender. Serve the curry hot with Soft Kachori, rice or chapattis.

SOFT
KACHORI

Most of us know kachori as small, crispy, pocket-shaped snacks, but there is a soft version that's very popular in Kolkata, where it's eaten with Potato, Paneer and Chickpea Curry (*see* page 60) at any time of day, although soft kachori are great to eat on their own, too. *See* photograph, page 60.

For the dough
200g (7oz) plain flour
4 teaspoons sunflower oil,
   plus extra for deep-frying
1/2 teaspoon salt
about 6 tablespoons water

For the filling
125g (41/2oz) split black lentils
   (urad dal)
200ml (1/3 pint) boiling water
40g (11/2oz) semolina
1/2 teaspoon baking powder
pinch of asafoetida
1/4 teaspoon salt
1/2 teaspoon cumin seeds
1/2 teaspoon carom seeds

To make the dough, combine the flour, oil and salt in a bowl. Mix in just enough of the measured water, adding it 1 tablespoon at a time, to form a soft dough. Put the dough into a bowl, cover the bowl with clingfilm and leave to rest until the filling is ready.

To make the filling, put the lentils into a bowl, add the measured boiling water and leave to soak for 30 minutes. After the soaking time has elapsed, tip the lentils and water into a food processor or blender and blend roughly. Add the remaining filling ingredients and blend until well mixed.

Divide both the dough and filling into 8 equal portions. Roll out each portion of dough into a circle with a diameter of 5–8cm (2–31/4 inches). Spoon 1 portion of the filling into the centre of 1 dough circle, then fold up the dough from all sides to conceal the filling and press well to seal. Carefully roll out this parcel into a circle with a diameter of 7–10cm (23/4–4 inches). Repeat with the remaining portions of dough and filling.

Heat enough oil for deep-frying in a deep-fat fryer or large saucepan (ensuring the pan is no more than one-third full) to 190°C (375°F). Fry the kachori, 1 at a time, for about 2–3 minutes on each side, until golden brown. Serve hot.

CHANA DAL
WITH LUCHI

My childhood friend Sujana, who lives in Kolkata, cooked this luchi
for me when I visited her. It is a beautiful combination of fried
flatbreads and lentils cooked with coconut. In Kolkata, the luchi
are fried fresh and served piping hot. *See* photograph, page 65.

Tomato and Date Chutney
  (*see* page 220), to serve

For the dal
400g (14oz) split chickpeas
  (chana dal)
1.2 litres (2 pints) water
2 teaspoons salt
1/2 teaspoon ground turmeric
1 tablespoon sunflower or
  vegetable oil
1 cinnamon stick
1 bay leaf
1/2 teaspoon chilli powder
1 teaspoon cumin seeds
1 teaspoon mustard seeds
6 tablespoons freshly grated
  or desiccated coconut, plus
  extra to garnish

For the luchi
400g (14oz) plain flour, plus extra
  for dusting
about 150ml (1/4 pint) warm water
sunflower oil, for deep-frying

For the dal, put the split
chickpeas, measured water,
salt and turmeric into a deep
saucepan and simmer for
about 1 hour, until the split
chickpeas are fully cooked.

Meanwhile, start making the
luchi. Put the flour into a bowl
and gradually add just enough
(or a little more, if necessary) of
the measured warm water to
form a soft dough. Knead the
dough on a floured surface for
2 minutes, then put the dough
into a bowl, cover it with a tea
towel and leave it to rest for at
least 15 minutes.

When the split chickpeas are
cooked, heat the oil in a large
saucepan. Add the cinnamon
stick, bay leaf, chilli powder
and the cumin and mustard
seeds and cook for 1 minute,
until the spices begin to sizzle.
Stir in the coconut and cook
for 1 minute, then tip in the
cooked chickpeas. Mix well
and bring to a boil. Keep the
dal warm over low heat until
ready to serve.

Heat enough oil for deep-
frying in a deep-fat fryer or
large saucepan (ensuring the
pan is no more than one-third
full) to 180°C (350°F). Line a
plate with some kitchen paper.

Divide the dough into pieces
the size of a small lime. Roll
them out on a lightly floured
surface into 8-cm (3¹/4-inch)
circles. Fry the dough circles,
1 at a time, over medium heat
for 2 minutes, turning once,
until light golden. Transfer the
cooked luchi to the paper-
lined plate to drain excess oil.

Garnish the dal with extra
coconut and serve with the hot
flatbreads and the Tomato and
Date Chutney.

MOONG DAL
WITH CASHEWS

This special lentil dish from Kolkata is prepared in a way that
is very different to how I would normally cook moong dal.
I had to learn this recipe because I absolutely loved it served
in a thali with rice and fried fish when I was visiting the city.
Serve this dish hot with rice and Fish Fry (*see* page 78)
or enjoy the dal on its own as a bowl of soup.

300g (10½oz) split yellow lentils
  (moong dal)
1.4 litres (2½ pints) water
1 teaspoon salt
½ teaspoon ground turmeric
40g (1½oz) cashew nuts
1 tablespoon ghee
1 teaspoon cumin seeds
2.5cm (1 inch) piece of fresh root
  ginger, finely chopped
1 tomato, finely chopped
1 small green chilli, finely chopped
handful of fresh coriander leaves,
  finely chopped

Put the lentils into a saucepan
with the measured water,
salt and turmeric. Bring to a
boil, then simmer for about
25–30 minutes, until the
lentils are cooked.

Meanwhile, soak the cashew
nuts in a bowl of warm water
for 30 minutes.

Heat the ghee in a frying pan
over medium heat. Add the
cumin seeds and, when they
begin to sizzle, add the ginger.
Drain the cashews, add them
to the ginger and fry for
2 minutes or until the nuts
are golden. Add the tomato
and chilli and cook for about
2–3 minutes, until they soften.
Stir in the coriander.

Tip the contents of the frying
pan into the cooked dal and
mix well. Serve immediately.

BAIGAN BHAJA

These pakoras are spiced with nothing other than salt, turmeric and chilli, yet the flavour is outstanding, no doubt due to the beautifully tender aubergine encased in a crisp, tasty coating. Pair them with Coriander and Spinach Chutney or Tomato Chutney.

1 aubergine
1/2 teaspoon salt
1/2 teaspoon chilli powder
sunflower oil, for deep-frying
sea salt flakes
Coriander and Spinach Chutney
    (see page 228) and/or Tomato
    Chutney (see page 225), to serve

For the batter
150g (51/2oz) gram (chickpea) flour
3/4 teaspoon salt
1/2 teaspoon chilli powder
1/2 teaspoon turmeric
about 300ml (1/2 pint) water

Cut the aubergine vertically into thin slices with a thickness of no more than 5mm (1/4 inch). Rub the flesh with the salt and chilli powder leave to stand for 10 minutes. (This helps to release excess moisture in the aubergine flesh.)

To make the batter, combine the gram flour, salt and spices in a bowl, then gradually add just enough of the measured water to form a smooth batter with a thin coating consistency.

Heat enough oil for deep-frying in a deep-fat fryer or large saucepan (ensuring the pan is no more than one-third full) to 190°C (375°F). Line a plate with some kitchen paper. Working with 1 slice of aubergine at a time, press it between 2 sheets of kitchen paper to extract excess moisture, then dip the slice in the batter, add it to the hot oil and fry for 1 minute on each side, until deep golden brown and crispy. Transfer to the paper-lined plate and leave to drain excess oil while you fry the remaining aubergine slices. Season with sea salt flakes and serve hot with your preferred chutney.

PANTARAS

I had never heard of pantaras before visiting Kolkata but
found them being rolled at super speed on street-side stalls,
ready for the lunchtime rush. Mine are filled with chicken,
but you can replace it with your own choice of minced meat.

1 tablespoon cornflour
2 tablespoons water
sunflower oil, for deep-frying
Sichuan Sauce (*see page 224*) or
    Coriander and Spinach Chutney
    (*see page 228*), to serve

For the pancakes
150g (5¹/₂oz) plain flour
1 teaspoon ground turmeric
¹/₂ teaspoon salt
2 large eggs
300ml (¹/₂ pint) water

For the filling
1 tablespoon sunflower oil
1 bay leaf
4 cloves
2 green cardamom pods
1 small cinnamon stick
1 onion, finely chopped
1 carrot, finely chopped
1 green pepper, finely chopped
300g (10¹/₂oz) minced chicken
¹/₂ teaspoon salt
¹/₂ teaspoon chilli powder

For the pancakes, put the flour, turmeric and salt into a mixing bowl. Add the eggs and water and whisk until smooth. Heat a non-stick frying pan over medium to low heat. Pour 50ml (2fl oz) of the batter into it and quickly spread it around to make a very thin pancake. Cook on each side for 20 seconds, then transfer to a plate. Repeat with the remaining batter to make 12 or so pancakes.

For the filling, heat the oil in a wide saucepan over medium heat. Add the bay leaf, cloves, cardamom and cinnamon and cook for a few seconds. Add the onion and cook for about 5 minutes, until softened. Mix in the carrot and pepper and cook for another minute, until combined. Stir in the minced chicken, salt and chilli powder and cook for 10 minutes, until the chicken is done. Leave to cool slightly, then remove the cinnamon stick.

In a cup, mix the cornflour with the water to make a thin paste. To assemble, lay a pancake on your work surface. Arrange 1¹/₂ tablespoons of the chicken mixture in a line just to one side of the centre of the pancake. Fold 1 edge of the pancake over either end of this filling. Brush a little cornflour paste on the edge of the pancake furthest away from the filling, then roll up from the opposite edge to encase the filling and make a tight cigar shape. Repeat with the remaining ingredients.

Heat enough oil for deep-frying the pantaras in a deep-fat fryer or heavy saucepan to 190°C (375°F). Line a plate with kitchen paper. Fry the rolls a few at a time for 2 minutes on each side, until crisp and golden. Transfer to the plate to drain while you fry the remaining rolls. Serve hot with Sichuan Sauce or Coriander and Spinach Chutney.

ALU BHATE

This simple potato sabji is particular to Kolkata thali, in which it is typically served alongside Mussori Dal (*see* opposite), Fish Fry (*see* page 78) and rice. Mustard oil is more commonly used for cooking in this region than elsewhere, so its distinctive flavour makes its mark on the cuisine. Everyone likes to put their own touch on this recipe – adding tomatoes, leaving out the onion or turmeric, adding more liquid so the dish is more like a curry... If you don't want to make a complete thali, serve this dish with any puri or kachori. *See* photograph, pages 76–77.

1 tablespoon mustard oil
1 onion, finely chopped
1 teaspoon salt, plus extra
  for seasoning
1/2 teaspoon chilli powder
1/2 teaspoon ground turmeric
2–3 tablespoons water
4 floury potatoes, boiled, peeled
  and lightly mashed

Heat the oil in a saucepan set over medium heat. Add the onion and cook for about 5 minutes, until it begins to soften. Stir in the salt, chilli, turmeric and measured water and cook for 1 minute, until well combined.

Add the mashed potatoes to the saucepan, mix well, then serve immediately.

MUSSORI DAL

The mix of masoor dal and toor dal is so simple yet so delicious. This is mostly served as part of a thali on the streets of Kolkata, accompanied by Alu Bhate (*see* opposite), Fish Fry (*see* page 78) and rice, but is also very comforting on its own as a bowl of soup *See* photograph, pages 76–77.

150g (5¹/₂oz) split pigeon peas (toor dal)
150g (5¹/₂oz) red lentils (masoor dal)
¹/₂ teaspoon ground turmeric
1 teaspoon salt
800ml (1¹/₂ pints) cold water
400ml (14fl oz) boiling water
1 tablespoon sunflower oil
1 teaspoon nigella seeds (kalonji)
1 small green chilli, finely chopped
1 tomato, finely chopped
¹/₂ teaspoon chilli powder

Put the split pigeon peas and lentils into a saucepan with the turmeric, salt and the measured cold water. Bring to a boil, then reduce the heat and simmer for 30 minutes, until cooked. Add the measured boiling water to the pan and mix well.

Heat the oil in a small frying pan set over medium heat, then add the nigella seeds. Once they start to sizzle, add the green chilli and tomato and cook for 2 minutes, until the tomato begins to soften.

Finally, stir the chilli powder into the pan, then tip this mixture, known as tadka, into the cooked dals. Mix well and serve immediately.

FISH FRY

This crispy, flavourful fried fish dish is a staple in **Kolkata**, where it's an essential part of the local thali and is eaten with lentils, potato and rice as a main meal, but it also makes a great snack. Coriander and garlic balance the peppery taste of the mustard oil in which the fish is fried. *See* photograph, pages 76–77.

½ teaspoon salt
½ teaspoon ground turmeric
¼ teaspoon chilli powder
1 medium sea bream, cleaned, gutted and cut into 6 pieces
2 handfuls of fresh coriander leaves, finely chopped
4 garlic cloves, finely chopped
2 small green chillies, finely chopped
4 tablespoons mustard oil
2 tablespoons lemon juice

Mix the salt, turmeric and chilli powder in a small bowl. Rub the spice mixture over the fish pieces, then put them into a bowl and leave to stand for 15 minutes.

Using a pestle and mortar, mash the coriander, garlic and green chilli to a paste. Smear it over the fish.

Heat the mustard oil in a frying pan set over medium heat. Just as it begins to smoke, add the fish pieces and cook for 2–3 minutes on each side, until golden and crisp. Sprinkle over the lemon juice. Serve immediately.

CHICKEN CHOP

I really enjoyed eating these delicious hot snacks in Kolkata and was fascinated to see that the chefs give each flavour of chop a different shape – egg chops are oval, fish chops are cylindrical, and chicken chops are flat. It makes it very easy to tell them apart.

1 tablespoon sunflower oil, plus extra for deep-frying
1 onion, finely chopped
1 small green chilli, finely chopped
2 garlic cloves, finely chopped
2.5cm (1 inch) piece of fresh root ginger, peeled and finely chopped
1 teaspoon salt
1/2 teaspoon ground coriander
1/2 teaspoon ground cumin
1 teaspoon garam masala
500g (1lb 2oz) minced chicken
2 floury potatoes, boiled, peeled and mashed
handful of fresh coriander leaves, finely chopped
Coriander and Spinach Chutney (see page 228) or Tomato Chutney (see page 225), to serve

For the coating
2 eggs, lightly beaten
100g (3 1/2 oz) golden breadcrumbs

Heat the sunflower oil in a saucepan over medium heat. Add the onion and chilli and cook for 5 minutes, until the onion softens. Add the garlic and ginger and cook for 2 minutes, then add the salt and spices and mix well. Stir in the minced chicken and remove the pan from the heat – you don't want to cook the chicken at this stage or it will not bind well.

Transfer the chicken mixture to a bowl. Add the mashed potatoes and coriander and mix well.

Divide the chicken mixture into 20 portions. Take 1 portion in your palm and shape it into an oval. Press gently to flatten it a little. Dip the patty in the beaten egg, then roll it in breadcrumbs until coated. Repeat until you've used up all the chicken mixture.

Fill a deep-fat fryer or large saucepan with enough oil for deep-frying (ensuring the pan is no more than one-third full). Slowly heat the oil to 190°C (375°F). Line a plate with some kitchen paper. When the oil is hot, fry the chicken chops, a few at a time, for 2–3 minutes, turning halfway through, until golden brown. Transfer to the paper-lined plate and leave to drain excess oil while you cook the remaining chicken ovals. Serve hot with chutney.

FISH CHOP

These delicious fish chops from the streets of Kolkata
can be enjoyed hot or cold with a variety of chutneys.
If you want something fiery, try them with Sichuan Sauce;
if you'd prefer something mild, opt for Coriander and
Spinach Chutney.

3 large eggs
300g (10¹/₂oz) skinless cod fillets
1 onion, finely chopped
handful of fresh coriander leaves,
    finely chopped
2 garlic cloves, finely chopped
2 small green chillies, finely
    chopped
¹/₂ teaspoon salt
sunflower oil, for deep-frying
sea salt flakes
Sichuan Sauce (see page 224) or
    Coriander and Spinach Chutney
    (see page 228), to serve

For the coating
2 eggs, lightly beaten
100g (3¹/₂oz) golden breadcrumbs

Put the large eggs into a small saucepan, cover with water and boil for 10 minutes. Drain and leave to cool, then shell the eggs and mash them in a bowl.

In a food processor, blitz the cod to a coarse paste. Add the fish to the mashed eggs, along with the onion, coriander, garlic, chillies and salt. Mix thoroughly so that the flavours are well combined.

Shape the mixture into 15 balls about the size of a lemon, then press to flatten them slightly. Dip each one in the beaten egg, then roll them in the breadcrumbs until fully coated.

Heat enough oil for deep-frying in a deep-fat fryer or heavy saucepan (ensuring the pan is no more than one-third full) to 170–180°C (340–350°F). Line a plate with some kitchen paper. Fry the chops a few at a time for about 2 minutes, until they are cooked through and golden. Transfer to the paper-lined plate and leave to drain excess oil while you fry the remaining chops.

Season with sea salt flakes and serve warm with your choice of sauce or chutney.

EGG CHOPS

Think of these as Indian Scotch eggs – hard-boiled eggs covered with a spicy potato mixture, then coated in breadcrumbs and deep-fried. Crisp and delicious, they are very popular on the streets of Kolkata. Enjoy them with a green or red chutney of your choice.

4 large eggs
1 tablespoon sunflower oil
1 teaspoon cumin seeds
1 small green chilli, finely chopped
1 onion, finely chopped
2.5cm (1 inch) piece of fresh
    root ginger, peeled and
    finely chopped
2 garlic cloves, finely chopped
1/2 teaspoon salt
1/2 teaspoon chilli powder
1 teaspoon garam masala
4 floury potatoes, boiled, peeled
    and mashed
sunflower oil, for deep-frying
sea salt flakes
green or red chutney of your
    choice, to serve

For the coating
1 egg, lightly beaten
100g (3 1/2 oz) golden breadcrumbs

Boil the eggs for 12 minutes, then drain and set aside to cool.

Heat the sunflower oil in a large saucepan over medium heat. Add the cumin seeds and, once they begin to sizzle, add the green chilli and onion and cook for about 5 minutes, until the onion begins to soften. Add the ginger and garlic and cook for 1 minute, until fragrant, then add the salt, chilli powder and garam masala. Mix well, then mix in the mashed potato. Transfer the mixture to a bowl and set aside to cool.

Divide the cooled potato mixture into 8 equal portions. Shell the eggs, then cut them in half lengthways. Cover each egg half with a portion of the potato mixture, spreading and smoothing it over the surface of the egg to enclose it completely and give them a nice shape. Then dip each coated egg half in the beaten egg for the coating and roll it in the breadcrumbs until thoroughly coated.

Heat enough oil for deep-frying the egg halves in a deep-fat fryer or large saucepan pan (ensuring the pan is no more than one-third full) to 190°C (375°F) – it's important not to put the coated eggs into oil that is cooler than this temperature or they will break up. Line a plate with some kitchen paper. When the oil is hot, fry the egg chops, 1 at a time, turning gently, for about 3–4 minutes, until the coating is golden brown. Transfer to the paper-lined plate and leave to drain excess oil while you cook the remaining coated eggs. Season with sea salt flakes and serve hot with chutney.

CHICKEN STEW

Light yet comforting and super-delicious, this is known
as chicken ishtup on the streets of Kolkata, where it's
a much-loved lunch dish. You'll find it quite straightforward
to make at home, and just as heartening.

2 tablespoons sunflower oil
4 skinless chicken legs
4 garlic cloves, finely chopped
2.5cm (1 inch) piece of fresh
    root ginger, peeled and
    finely chopped
2 onions, finely chopped
6 tablespoons freshly grated
    coconut
1 litre (1³/4 pints) boiling water
1½ teaspoons salt
½ teaspoon ground turmeric
2 carrots, diced
2 floury potatoes, peeled and diced
1 tablespoon plain flour
½ teaspoon ground black pepper

Heat the oil in a wide saucepan over high heat. Cook the chicken pieces 1 at a time to avoid overcrowding the pan. Fry for about 5–10 minutes, turning to give them a lovely golden colour all over. Set aside.

Put the garlic, ginger and onions into the same saucepan used to cook the chicken pieces and cook over medium heat for 2 minutes, until the onion begins to soften, then add the coconut and return the fried chicken to the pan. Pour in the measured boiling water and add the salt and turmeric. Mix well, then cover the pan with a lid and simmer over low heat for 40 minutes, until the chicken is cooked.

Add the diced carrots and potatoes to the saucepan, cover the pan with a lid, and cook gently for a further 15 minutes, until softened.

Mix the flour with about 4–5 tablespoons of liquid from the stew in a small bowl to make a smooth paste. Stir this into the stew, then bring to a boil and cook over high heat for 2 minutes, until slightly thickened. Serve piping hot with the pepper sprinkled over.

EGG KATHI
ROLL

On the streets of **Kolkata**, these hot wrap-style sandwiches are served deep-fried. With this recipe **I**'ve tried to make a healthier option that tastes just as amazing – no easy task! But this version is lighter, fresh and very satisfying. *See* photograph, pages 90–91.

For the flatbreads
100g (3¹/₂oz) plain flour,
   plus extra for dusting
50g (1³/₄oz) chapatti flour
about 6 tablespoons water
6 eggs
12 teaspoons sunflower oil

For the filling
1 tablespoon sunflower oil
4 onions, thinly sliced
1 green chilli, finely chopped
¹/₄ teaspoon salt
¹/₄ teaspoon Chaat Masala
   (*see* page 230)
Chilli and Garlic Chutney
   (*see* page 229)
1 onion, finely chopped
handful of fresh coriander leaves,
   finely chopped

To make the flatbreads, put the flours into a bowl. Gradually mix in just enough of the measured water (or a little more, if necessary) to form a dough. Knead the dough on a lightly floured surface for 2 minutes, then put the dough into a bowl, cover the bowl with clingfilm and leave to rest for 15 minutes.

To make the filling, heat the oil in a frying pan over medium heat. Add the onion and cook, stirring occasionally, for about 10 minutes, until golden brown. Stir in the chilli, salt and Chaat Masala, then set aside.

To cook the flatbreads, heat a frying pan over medium heat. Divide the dough into 6 equal portions. Roll out 1 portion into a circle with a diameter of roughly 17–18cm (6¹/₂–7 inches). Cook the first dough circle in the hot frying pan for 1 minute on each side, until the dough starts to change colour. Whisk 1 of the eggs in a bowl and pour it on top of the flatbread. Turn it over and pour 1 teaspoon oil around the edges of the flatbread. Cook for about 2 minutes, until the egg is done, then turn again, pour another teaspoon oil around the edges of the flatbread and cook for 2 minutes, until golden brown.

Transfer the cooked egg flatbread to a serving plate. Spoon some of the spicy cooked onions on top. Drizzle with a little Chilli and Garlic Chutney, then add some raw onion and coriander. Roll up the flatbread to secure the filling and serve. Repeat with the remaining portions of dough and filling ingredients.

CHICKEN KATHI ROLL

Originally from Kolkata, these spicy and delicious flatbread rolls are now found all over India. **The chicken can be barbecued, shallow-fried or baked.** *See* photograph, pages 90–91.

For the flatbreads
100g (3¹/₂oz) plain flour, plus extra for dusting
50g (1³/₄oz) chapatti flour
about 6 tablespoons water
12 teaspoons sunflower oil

For the filling
50g (1³/₄oz) natural yogurt
¹/₂ teaspoon salt
¹/₂ teaspoon chilli powder
¹/₂ teaspoon garam masala
¹/₂ teaspoon ground turmeric
¹/₂ teaspoon ground cumin
300g (10¹/₂oz) chicken breast, cut into 1cm (¹/₂ inch) dice
1 tablespoon sunflower oil
5 onions, 4 thinly sliced and 1 finely chopped
1 green chilli, finely chopped
¹/₄ teaspoon salt
¹/₄ teaspoon Chaat Masala (see page 230)
Coriander and Spinach Chutney (see page 228)

To prepare the filling, put the yogurt, salt and spices into a bowl, then stir in the chicken cubes. Cover with clingfilm and leave to marinate for at least 30 minutes, but ideally overnight. If marinating the chicken for more than 1 hour, leave it in the refrigerator.

For the flatbreads, put the flours into a bowl. Gradually mix in just enough of the measured water to form a dough. Knead on a lightly floured surface for 2 minutes, then place in a bowl, cover with clingfilm and leave to rest for 15 minutes.

To cook the chicken, preheat the oven to 200°C (400°F), Gas Mark 6. Lift the chicken pieces out of the marinade, spread them out on a roasting tray and roast for 20 minutes.

To finish the filling, heat the oil in a frying pan over medium heat. Add the sliced onion and cook, stirring occasionally, for 10 minutes, until golden brown.

Stir in the chilli, salt and Chaat Masala, then add the cooked chicken and mix well. Set aside.

To cook the flatbreads, heat a frying pan over medium heat. Divide the dough into 6 equal portions. Roll out 1 portion into a circle with a diameter of 17–18cm (6¹/₂–7 inches). Cook the first dough circle in the hot frying pan for 1 minute on each side, until it starts to change colour. Pour 1 teaspoon oil across the top of the flatbread, then turn it over and cook for 2 minutes, until golden. Drizzle 1 teaspoon oil across the uncooked surface, turn over the flatbread and cook this side for 2 minutes, until golden.

Transfer the cooked flatbread to a serving plate. Spoon some of the filling on top, drizzle with Coriander and Spinach Chutney and add a little raw chopped onion. Roll it up and serve it hot. Repeat with the remaining portions of dough and the filling ingredients.

DAL CHILLA

Chilla – light and healthy savoury pancakes –
are a popular snack in Kolkata and many other parts
of India. They taste wonderful with Coriander and
Spinach Chutney (*see* page 228) or Chilli and Garlic Chutney
(*see* page 229), and with dal or a potato curry. Try making
them with different varieties of lentils, if you like.

sunflower oil, for cooking
chutney of your choice, to serve

For the batter
250g (9oz) split yellow lentils
  (moong dal)
600ml (20fl oz) water
2.5cm (1 inch) fresh root ginger,
  peeled and roughly chopped
1 small green chilli
handful of coriander leaves
1 teaspoon salt
50g (1¾oz) semolina

For the topping
1 large onion, finely chopped
¼ teaspoon salt
1 green chilli, finely chopped

To make the batter, soak the lentils in 250ml (9fl oz) of the measured water for about 1 hour, until they absorb it all.

Transfer the lentils to a blender and add the ginger, chilli, and coriander and blend until smooth. Tip the paste into a bowl and stir in the salt, semolina and the remaining 350ml (12fl oz) measured water, mixing well.

Combine all the topping ingredients in a bowl.

To cook the chilla, heat a frying pan and, once it is very hot, pour a serving-spoonful of the batter into the pan and spread it into a 13–15-cm (5–6-inch) circle. Top with 1 tablespoon of the topping mixture and drizzle 1 tablespoon of oil around the edges of the batter. Cook over medium heat for 2–3 minutes, until golden brown on the underside, then turn the chilla over and cook for a further 2 minutes, until golden brown on both sides. Repeat to make 15 more.

Serve hot with the chutney of your choice.

CHICKEN
LOLLIPOPS

Having eaten chicken lollipops in Mumbai, Kolkata and Delhi,
I'm aware that there are a few different versions of this dish
– sometimes, chicken wings are used instead of drumsticks, or
the chicken is breadcrumbed rather than battered. This recipe
is for the version I find tastiest, which I had in Kolkata.

sunflower oil, for deep-frying
sea salt flakes
Sichuan Sauce (*see page 224*),
   to serve

For the chicken
8 small skinless chicken drumsticks
1 tablespoon soy sauce
1 tablespoon chilli-garlic sauce
1/2 teaspoon salt
1/4 teaspoon ground black pepper

For the batter
150g (5 1/2oz) plain flour
2 tablespoons cornflour
1/2 teaspoon salt
1/4 teaspoon ground black pepper
1 tablespoon chilli sauce
1 tablespoon ketchup
200ml (1/3 pint) water

To prepare the chicken, take 1 drumstick and cut the base of the muscle that holds the meat to the bone at the hock. Stand the drumstick on its other end and push the meat downwards to expose the bone. This is what gives it the lollipop appearance. Repeat with the remaining drumsticks.

Put the drumsticks into a bowl with the soy sauce, chilli-garlic sauce, salt and pepper and turn to coat evenly. Leave to marinate for at least 1 hour or, ideally, overnight – if you marinate the chicken for more than 1 hour, put it into the refrigerator.

To make the batter, combine all the ingredients, except the water, in a bowl. Add the measured water gradually, stirring constantly, until the mixture is smooth.

Fill a deep-fat fryer or a large saucepan with enough oil for deep-frying (ensuring the pan is no more than one-third full) and heat it to 180°C (350°F). Line a plate with some kitchen paper. Dip 1 drumstick into the batter and carefully drop it into the hot oil. Fry for 3–4 minutes on each side, until the batter is golden brown and the chicken is cooked through. Transfer to the paper-lined plate and leave to drain excess oil while you dip and fry the remaining drumsticks. Season with sea salt flakes and serve hot with Sichuan Sauce.

EGG CURRY

Perhaps the most delicious of all curries, egg curry
features a simple yet brilliant combination of flavours.
Versions of it can be found in many regions of India, each
with their own interesting twist, but I especially love the one
I ate in Kolkata, where they fried the boiled eggs to give them
a bit of colour and served them in a delicious coconut sauce.
Here is my take on this tasty dish. For a healthier option,
simply omit frying the boiled eggs.

4 tablespoons sunflower oil
1 small cinnamon stick
1 bay leaf
4 green cardamom pods
4 onions, grated or minced
  to a paste
2.5cm (1 inch) piece of fresh
  root ginger, peeled and
  finely chopped
4 garlic cloves, finely chopped
400g (14oz) can chopped tomatoes
1 1/2 teaspoons salt
1 teaspoon granulated sugar
2 teaspoons ground coriander
1 teaspoon garam masala
1/2 teaspoon ground turmeric
400ml (14fl oz) coconut milk
100ml (3 1/2fl oz) boiling water
8 large eggs
rice or puri, to serve (optional)

Heat 2 tablespoons of the oil in
a wide saucepan over medium
heat. Add the cinnamon, bay
leaf and cardamom and cook
for 1 minute, until fragrant,
then add the onions and cook
over medium heat until they
are a dark golden brown – this
could take up to 30 minutes.

When the onions have
browned, stir in the ginger
and garlic and cook for
another 2 minutes, until they
begin to soften, then add the
canned tomatoes. Mix well,
reduce the heat to low, cover
the pan with a lid and cook for
15 minutes, until the tomatoes
are cooked.

Add the salt, sugar, coriander,
garam masala and turmeric
to the pan, mix well and cook
for 2 minutes, then stir in the
coconut milk and measured
boiling water. Cover the
pan with a lid and cook for
5–10 minutes, until the sauce
is slightly thickened.

Meanwhile, boil the eggs
in a separate saucepan for
10 minutes, then drain and
cool under running cold
water. Shell the boiled eggs.

Heat the remaining oil in a
saucepan and fry the whole
boiled eggs for 2 minutes over
high heat, turning occasionally,
until golden. Pop the eggs in
the curry and serve hot with
some rice or puri, if liked.

SIMPLE FISH CURRY

I tried this quick and easy curry in **Kolkata** as part
of a thali and managed to get the recipe from my friend
Sujana, who cooks it often at home. It makes a great
mid-week meal when you're pushed for time but you still
want something truly delicious. Serve with **Alu Bhate**
(*see* page 74) and rice for a full meal.

1 large onion
2.5cm (1 inch) piece of fresh
  root ginger, peeled
1 small green chilli
2 tablespoons mustard oil
3/4 teaspoon salt
1/2 teaspoon chilli powder
1/2 teaspoon ground coriander
1/2 teaspoon garam masala
1/2 teaspoon ground cumin
1/2 teaspoon ground turmeric
1/2 teaspoon granulated sugar
550g (1lb 4oz) halibut, cut into
  5cm (2 inch) pieces
200ml (1/3 pint) boiling water
50ml (2fl oz) natural yogurt

Put the onion, ginger and
green chilli into a blender or
small food processor and blend
the mixture to a paste.

Heat the oil in a wide saucepan
and, once it starts to smoke,
add the onion paste. Cook
over medium-low heat for
10–15 minutes, stirring often,
until golden brown.

Once the onion paste has
browned, stir in the salt,
spices and sugar and cook for
1 minute, until well combined.
Add the fish pieces and
mix well, then pour in the
measured boiling water and
cook for 2–3 minutes, until
the fish begins to cook.

Gently stir the yogurt into
the curry, being careful not
to break the fish pieces. Cook
for another 3–4 minutes, or
until the fish is done. Serve
immediately.

AUBERGINE
CURRY

This recipe features a lovely combination of spices that is typical of **Kolkata** cooking, including mustard and also panch phoron, a blend of mustard, cumin, onion, fenugreek and fennel seeds that is perhaps best known for its use in **Bengali** food. Also known as baigan curry, this dish is served as an element of thali at some street stalls. It is also delicious when enjoyed simply with rice or chapatti. *See* photograph, page 103.

1 large aubergine, cut into chunky pieces roughly 5cm (2 inch) long
1/2 teaspoon salt
1/2 teaspoon ground turmeric
1 tablespoon sunflower oil, plus extra for deep frying
1 teaspoon panch phoron
1 large onion, finely chopped
1 small green chilli, finely chopped
1cm (1/2 inch) piece of fresh root ginger, peeled and finely chopped
2 garlic cloves, finely chopped
1/2 teaspoon granulated sugar
1 teaspoon English mustard
4 tablespoons natural yogurt
4 tablespoons water
handful of fresh coriander leaves, finely chopped

Put the aubergine pieces into a bowl and sprinkle over 1/4 teaspoon each of the salt and turmeric. Set aside for 1 hour to extract the excess moisture.

Heat enough oil for deep-frying in a deep-fat fryer or heavy saucepan (ensuring the pan is no more than one-third full) to 190°C (375°F). Line a plate with some kitchen paper.

Wipe the excess moisture from the aubergine pieces using kitchen paper. When the oil has reached the correct temperature, carefully add the aubergine pieces in small batches and fry for 2 minutes, until they are golden. Transfer to the paper-lined plate and leave to drain excess oil while you fry the remaining aubergine pieces.

Heat 1 tablespoon sunflower oil in a saucepan over medium heat and add the panch phoron. Cook for a few seconds to release the aromas, then add the onion and chilli and cook for about 3–4 minutes, until the onion is golden brown. Stir in the ginger and garlic and cook for 2 minutes. Then add the remaining salt and turmeric, the sugar and the mustard and mix well. Continue to cook for 1 minute, then stir in the yogurt and measured water, increase the heat to high and cook for 2 minutes, until the mixture begins to thicken.

Add the fried aubergine pieces to the curry, then cover the pan with a lid and simmer for 5 minutes. Transfer the curry to a serving bowl, sprinkle over the coriander and serve hot.

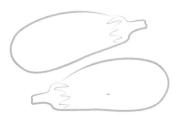

MALAI
PRAWN CURRY

Malai means cream, and this delicious curry
gets its creaminess from coconut milk and a paste made
from cashews and fennel seeds. My friend Sujana, who lives
in Kolkata, passed on the recipe to me. What's interesting
about this dish is that people eat the whole prawn, including
the head, which is very juicy. I did try, but found I couldn't!
But despite that, this is one of the most delicious
seafood curries I have ever eaten.

20g (³/₄oz) cashew nuts
1 teaspoon fennel seeds
3 tablespoons milk
1 tablespoon sunflower oil
1 onion, grated
1/2 teaspoon salt
1/2 teaspoon chilli powder
1/2 teaspoon ground turmeric
1/2 teaspoon garam masala
200ml (1/3 pint) coconut milk
50ml (2fl oz) water
12 raw peeled prawns
rice, to serve (optional)

Soak the cashews and fennel seeds in the milk for 1 hour. Once the soaking time has elapsed, transfer the milk, nuts and seeds to a food processor or blender and blend them to a fine paste. Set aside.

Heat the oil in a saucepan over medium heat. Add the onion and cook for 10–15 minutes, until deep golden brown. Stir in the salt and spices and cook for 2 minutes, then add the coconut milk and measured water and mix well.

Add the prawns and cook gently for 5 minutes. Stir in the cashew paste and cook for a further 5 minutes or until the prawns are cooked through. Serve piping hot with rice, if liked.

MUMBAI

Mumbai will always be close to my heart. I'm still fascinated by its vibrancy – all the stuff being sold in shops, hanging outside the doors, and everyone running around trying to make a living. There is no escape from people, but every face here tells a different story.

Mumbai is the one city in which you can find street food from the crack of dawn until beyond midnight. You are never far from it. While the Maharashtrian capital has the best vada pav (deep-fried spiced potato patties in a soft bread roll) I have ever eaten, it's not to be found at just one stall: in this city, every area has a famous vada pav stall.

And just as some popular Mumbai dishes are enjoyed all over the world, the city has brought in foods from other places and made them its own. I'm thinking of the city's take on Chinese cuisine, for example, the huge variety of dosa that are so different to the authentic versions from Chennai, and Mumbai's papdi chaat, which is drier, crunchier and spicier than that of Delhi.

I always notice that the people selling this inventive street food for their livelihood have such happy faces. They make their specialities with great love and care and are delighted to talk about their recipes and dishes to the many customers who stop by to have a laugh and enjoy the food.

There is some authentic Maharashtrian food available in the city, but it's not found in the popular foodie areas. I do wish there were more of these traditional dishes to be found amid Mumbai's street stalls – it would be marvellous.

PAPDI CHAAT

My all-time favourite chaat recipe is made in minutes
if you have some papdi ready (papdi will keep for at least
2–3 weeks in an airtight box). There are, of course, variations
of this famous street food snack available in every Indian city
but this is my mum's way of preparing it.

sunflower oil, for deep-frying

For the papdi
100g (3½oz) plain flour
¼ teaspoon salt
¼ teaspoon chilli powder
¼ teaspoon carom seeds
1 teaspoon sunflower oil
4–5 tablespoons water

For the chaat
300ml (½ pint) natural yogurt
4 tablespoons water
2 teaspoons salt, plus extra
   for sprinkling
2 floury potatoes, boiled, peeled
   and finely chopped
1 teaspoon chilli powder
1 teaspoon Chaat Masala
   (see page 230)
6 teaspoons Mint Chutney
   (see page 228)
6 teaspoons Tamarind Chutney
   (see page 220)
handful of fine gram flour
   noodles (sev)

To make the papdi, combine
the flour, salt, chilli and carom
in a bowl. Stir in the oil, then
slowly add the measured
water to form a dough. Cover
the bowl with clingfilm and
leave the dough to rest for
30 minutes.

Fill a deep-fat fryer or heavy
saucepan with enough oil for
deep-frying (ensuring the pan
is no more than one-third
full). Line a plate with some
kitchen paper. Heat the oil to
190°C (375°F). Meanwhile, take
small portions of the rested
dough, each roughly the size
of a grape, and roll them out
into about 30 small, thin circles
with a diameter of about 5cm
(2 inches).

Working in small batches, fry
the papdi, a few at a time, for
2–3 minutes, until golden.
Transfer to the paper-lined
plate and leave to drain
and cool while you fry the
remaining dough.

For the chaat, mix the yogurt
with the measured water and
salt in a small bowl.

When ready to eat, place
5 papdi on each serving plate.
Divide the chopped potato
between them and sprinkle
each with a pinch of salt.
Spoon 2–3 tablespoons of
the yogurt mixture over each
serving and dust with chilli
powder, Chaat Masala and
a pinch of salt. Drizzle with
1 teaspoon Mint Chutney
followed by 1 teaspoon
Tamarind Chutney. Sprinkle
with noodles to finish and
serve immediately.

HOT AND SPICY
CHILLI CHICKEN

Chilli chicken is very popular in India, where it is mostly eaten with fried rice or chow mein. Beware – this is one hot dish! Feel free to tone down the heat according to your liking. Replace the chicken with paneer if you are looking for a vegetarian option.

sunflower oil, for deep-frying
rice or Vegetable Chow Mein
   (see page 119), to serve
   (optional)

For the marinated chicken
50g (1³/₄oz) plain flour
10g (¹/₄oz) cornflour
¹/₂ teaspoon salt
¹/₂ teaspoon chilli sauce
1 teaspoon soy sauce
2.5cm (1 inch) piece of fresh root
   ginger, peeled and grated
2 garlic cloves, grated
2 large eggs, whisked
2 tablespoons water
500g (1lb 2 oz) chicken breasts,
   cut into 2.5cm (1 inch) pieces

For the sauce
2 tablespoons sunflower oil
4 garlic cloves, grated
2 small green chillies, halved
2.5cm (1 inch) piece of fresh root
   ginger, peeled and grated
5 red onions, thinly sliced
1 green pepper, thinly sliced
1 tablespoon dark soy sauce
1 teaspoon rice wine vinegar
1 tablespoon chilli-garlic sauce
¹/₂ teaspoon salt
2 tablespoons water

To prepare the chicken, combine the flours, salt, chilli sauce, soy sauce, ginger, garlic, eggs and measured water in a bowl to make a marinade and add the chicken pieces. Cover and leave to marinate for 1 hour.

Heat enough oil for deep-frying in a deep-fat fryer or heavy saucepan (ensuring the pan is no more than one-third full) to 180°C (350°F). Once the oil reaches that temperature, remove the chicken pieces from the marinade and fry, in batches, for 3–4 minutes, until golden brown.

To make the sauce, heat the sunflower oil in a wide saucepan set over medium heat. Add the garlic, green chillies and ginger and cook for 1 minute, until fragrant, then add the onions and cook for about 8–10 minutes, until golden brown.

Stir in the green pepper and cook for 1 minute, then add the soy sauce, vinegar, chilli-garlic sauce, salt and measured water. Mix well.

Add the fried chicken pieces to the sauce and give it a good stir. Serve hot with rice or chow mein, if liked.

OMELETTE
PAV

In Mumbai, eggs are cooked with spices and served with chutney inside a bread roll. It's such a simple combination but tastes amazing, and it makes a great quick meal. *See* photograph, pages 116–117.

1 teaspoon sunflower oil
1/2 onion, finely chopped
1/2 green chilli, finely chopped
1/2 tomato, finely chopped
large pinch of salt
large pinch of pepper
large pinch of garam masala
2 eggs
Coriander and Spinach Chutney
  (*see* page 228)
1 small soft bread roll (pav),
  split horizontally
sea salt flakes

Heat 1/2 a teaspoon of the sunflower oil in a small frying pan over medium heat. Add the onion and chilli and cook for about 5 minutes, until the onion is soft. Add the tomato and cook for 2 minutes, until the tomatoes begin to soften. Stir in the salt, pepper and garam masala.

Whisk the eggs together in a bowl and tip the cooked onion masala into it, mixing well.

Heat the remaining oil in the same frying pan and pour in the egg mixture. Cook over low to medium heat for 1 minute on each side, until the egg is cooked. Fold the omelette in half, then fold it in half again.

Spread some chutney on 1 side of the bread roll. Place the folded omelette on top, season with sea salt flakes, and close the bun. Serve hot.

VADA PAV

Perfect for breakfast, lunch or dinner, vada pav are ubiquitous in Mumbai. When living in the city I used to have them all the time – they are so readily available, delicious and make a good, cheap meal to eat on the go. *See* photograph, pages 116–117.

sunflower oil, for deep-frying
sea salt flakes

For the vada
1 tablespoon sunflower oil
1 teaspoon black mustard seeds
8 curry leaves
1 green chilli, finely chopped
1 garlic clove, finely chopped
15mm (5/8 inch) piece of fresh
    root ginger, peeled and finely
    chopped
1 teaspoon salt
1/4 teaspoon ground turmeric
3 floury potatoes, boiled, peeled
    and mashed

For the batter
100g (31/2oz) gram (chickpea) flour
1 teaspoon salt
1/4 teaspoon ground turmeric
about 100ml (31/2fl oz) water

To serve
10 small soft bread rolls (pav),
    split horizontally
Coriander and Spinach Chutney
    (*see* page 228)
Chilli and Garlic Chutney
    (*see* page 229)

To make the vada, heat the sunflower oil in a frying pan set over medium heat. Add the mustard seeds and, once they begin to pop, add the curry leaves, chilli, garlic, ginger, salt and turmeric. Mix well, then stir in the mashed potatoes. Cook for 2 minutes, until well combined, then set aside to cool.

Once cool, shape the spicy potato mixture into 10 balls.

To make the batter, combine the gram flour, salt and turmeric in a mixing bowl. Slowly stir in just enough of the water to give the mixture the consistency of crêpe batter.

Heat enough oil for deep-frying in a deep-fat fryer or heavy saucepan (ensuring the pan is no more than one-third full) to 180°C (350°F). Line a plate with some kitchen paper. Dip the potato balls in the batter and fry them, a few at a time, for 2 minutes on each side or until lightly golden. Transfer to the paper-lined plate to drain excess oil.

Spread Coriander and Spinach Chutney on 1 half of each bread roll and Chilli and Garlic Chutney on the other. Pop the piping-hot vada in the middle, season with sea salt flakes and serve hot. (Alternatively, simply enjoy the vada with the chutneys.)

VEGETABLE
CHOW MEIN

This is a great meal when freshly prepared on the streets of India – I used to eat loads of it when living in Mumbai. Chinese food is popular all over the country, but especially in Mumbai and Kolkata, and can be found in restaurants as well as street stalls. This dish is delicious on its own or, even better, with **Hot and Spicy Chilli Chicken** (*see* page 112) or **Vegetable Manchurian** (*see* page 155).

2 tablespoons sunflower oil
2.5cm (1 inch) piece of fresh root ginger, peeled and finely chopped
4 garlic cloves, finely chopped
2 small green chillies, finely chopped
1 red onion, thinly sliced
2 celery sticks, finely chopped
1 carrot, finely chopped
1 green pepper, finely chopped
4 spring onions, finely chopped, white and green parts kept separately
1½ teaspoons salt
½ teaspoon ground black pepper
1 tablespoon dark soy sauce
1 teaspoon rice wine vinegar
1 teaspoon chilli-garlic sauce
4 nests of medium-fine egg noodles, cooked according to the packet instructions

Heat the oil in a wide saucepan over medium heat. Add the ginger, garlic and chillies and cook for 1 minute, until fragrant. Stir in the red onion, celery, carrot, green pepper and finely chopped white parts of the spring onions and stir-fry for 5 minutes, until they begin to soften.

Stir the salt, black pepper, soy sauce, vinegar and chilli-garlic sauce into the pan and mix well. Add the cooked noodles and toss to combine. Sprinkle with the finely chopped green parts of the spring onions and serve immediately.

VEGETABLE
TOAST SANDWICH

One thing you don't want to miss when visiting Mumbai is this toasted sandwich filled with spicy potatoes, vegetables and chutney. It's so popular that it is now famous all over the country, and makes the perfect snack or light meal.

sea salt flakes

For the masala
1 teaspoon sunflower oil
1/4 teaspoon salt
1/4 teaspoon chilli powder
1/4 teaspoon garam masala
2 floury potatoes, boiled, peeled and mashed

For the sandwich
8 slices of white bread
salted butter, softened
1/2 cucumber, thinly sliced
1 cooked beetroot, thinly sliced
1 onion, thinly sliced
1 tomato, thinly sliced
Coriander and Spinach Chutney (see page 228)
salt

To make the masala, heat the oil in a small pan and add the salt, chilli and garam masala. Stir well, then add the mashed potatoes and mix until thoroughly combined. Remove from the heat and set aside.

To make the sandwiches, heat a sandwich toaster. Butter both sides of 1 slice of bread and place it in the sandwich maker. Add 2 tablespoons of the potato mixture and spread it out evenly. Top with a few slices of cucumber, followed by a little beetroot, onion and tomato. Season with a pinch of salt.

Take a second slice of bread and spread chutney over one side. Place it, with the chutney side facing downwards, on top of the tomato, then spread the top surface with butter. Close the machine and toast for about 2 minutes, or until golden brown. Repeat with the remaining ingredients. Season the toasted sandwiches with sea salt flakes and serve hot.

MISAL PAV

Hot and spicy, sour and sweet, finished beautifully with crunchy Bombay mix and served with buttery toasted rolls – I have loved this dish ever since I first tried it in Mumbai.

For the vegetable mixture
1 tablespoon sunflower oil
1 teaspoon cumin seeds
1/2 teaspoon mustard seeds
5 curry leaves
1 onion, finely chopped
1 small green chilli, finely chopped
2 garlic cloves, finely chopped
1cm (1/2 inch) piece of fresh root
   ginger, peeled and chopped
1 1/2 teaspoons salt
1 teaspoon ground coriander
1 teaspoon garam masala
1 teaspoon ground cumin
1 teaspoon tamarind paste
1 teaspoon granulated sugar
400ml (14fl oz) boiling water
1 floury potato, boiled, peeled
   and diced
1 tomato, diced
400g (14oz) can three-bean salad,
   drained (or use 250g/9oz cooked
   mixed beans)

For the pav
4 teaspoons salted butter
4 small soft bread rolls (pav),
   split horizontally

To garnish
lemon juice
handful of fresh coriander leaves,
   finely chopped
1 onion, finely chopped
handful of Bombay mix

For the vegetable mixture, heat the oil in a pan over medium heat. Add the cumin and mustard seeds and, once they begin to pop, add the curry leaves, onion and chilli and cook for 6–8 minutes, until the onion is golden brown. Add the garlic and ginger and cook for 2 minutes more.

Stir in all the salt, spices, tamarind paste and sugar and cook for 1 minute, until well combined. Pour in the measured boiling water, then add the diced potato, tomato and beans. Cover the pan and cook for 5 minutes, until the sauce begins to thicken.

To cook the pav, heat the butter in a frying pan over medium heat. Lay the bread rolls in the pan with the cut sides facing downwards and cook for about 2 minutes, until golden brown.

Serve the vegetable mixture in a bowl. Squeeze over a tiny bit of lemon juice, then scatter over the coriander leaves, chopped onion and Bombay mix. Serve hot with the buttered pav.

BHEL

Bhel is one of the most popular street foods of India.
It is available all over the country and is known by different
names in the various regions, including bhel puri and jhal muri.
It features a great combination of light, refreshing flavours yet
takes mere seconds to prepare once you have the ingredients to
hand. Feel free to add things you like and leave out anything
that's not to your taste. *See* photograph, pages 124–125.

100g (3½oz) puffed rice (kurmura)

100g (3½oz) gram flour noodles (sev)

10 papdi (*see* page 110), broken into pieces

handful of roasted peanuts

2 floury potatoes, boiled, peeled and finely chopped

1 onion, finely chopped

1 teaspoon Chaat Masala (*see* page 230)

½ teaspoon salt

2 tablespoons Tamarind Chutney (*see* page 220)

2 tablespoons Coriander and Spinach Chutney (*see* page 228)

1 tablespoon lemon juice

handful of fresh coriander leaves, finely chopped

Combine the puffed rice, noodles, papdi, peanuts, cooked potato, onion, Chaat Masala and salt in a large bowl and mix well.

Add the chutneys and lemon juice and mix again until the ingredients are evenly distributed. Serve immediately, sprinkled with the coriander.

DABELI

Originally from Gujarat, this dish is very popular in
Mumbai too, and was one of my favourite things to eat when
I lived in the city. It is essentially an extraordinary riot
of flavours and textures, with the sour and spicy chutneys,
the delicious potato mixture, and then the crunch of peanuts
and pomegranate. Years after leaving Mumbai I finally got my
hands on this recipe, which was given to me by a friend's mum.
It was worth the wait! *See* photograph, page 129.

For the potato mixture
2 tablespoons sunflower oil
1 tablespoon butter
1 onion, finely chopped
1 tomato, finely chopped
1 teaspoon salt
2 tablespoons Dabeli Masala
  (*see* page 233)
4 floury potatoes, boiled, peeled
  and mashed
1 tablespoon lime juice

For the chilli roast peanuts
150g (5½oz) peanuts
1 teaspoon sunflower oil
½ teaspoon salt
½ teaspoon chilli powder

To serve
6 small soft bread rolls (pav)
Tamarind Chutney (*see* page 220)
Chilli and Garlic Chutney
  (*see* page 229)
handful of pomegranate seeds
handful of fresh coriander leaves,
  finely chopped

For the potato, heat the oil and butter in a wide saucepan over medium heat. Add the onion and cook for about 5 minutes, until softened. Add the tomato and cook for 5 minutes, until the tomato softens, then stir in the salt and Dabeli Masala. Add the mashed potato and mix well, then stir in the lime juice. Set aside.

To prepare the chilli roast peanuts, put the peanuts and oil into a small saucepan and cook over low heat for about 2 minutes, until the nuts begin to change colour. Stir in the salt and chilli powder, then take the pan off the heat and leave to cool. Once cool, roughly crush the peanuts using a pestle and mortar.

To serve, cut the bread rolls in half, leaving them joined together at 1 end. Spread 1 teaspoon Tamarind Chutney on 1 half of each bread roll and ¼ teaspoon Chilli and Garlic Chutney on the other. Put around 2 tablespoons of the potato mixture in the middle of the lower half of the roll, and sprinkle over some peanuts, pomegranate and coriander leaves. Close the bread roll and eat straight away.

PAV BHAJI

This is another very popular dish from Mumbai, which is now found across India. My version is simple and healthy, but there are many other ways you could make it. When eaten on the streets, what makes this dish amazing is all the extra butter they put on the pav and bhaji, but I have tried to keep this to a minimum.

For the bhaji
2 tablespoons sunflower oil
1 tablespoon salted butter,
  plus extra as desired
1 onion, finely chopped
2 tomatoes, finely chopped
1/4 cauliflower (about 5–6 florets),
  grated
1 green pepper, finely chopped
600ml (20fl oz) water
1 1/2 teaspoons salt
2 tablespoons Pav Bhaji Masala
  (see page 233)
5 floury potatoes, boiled, peeled
  and grated
handful of fresh coriander,
  finely chopped

To serve
4 tablespoons butter
4 small soft bread rolls (pav),
  split horizontally
lime wedges

To make the bhaji, heat the oil and butter in a wide saucepan over medium heat. Add the onion and cook for about 5 minutes, until it begins to soften. Stir in the tomatoes, grated cauliflower, green pepper and 250ml (8fl oz) of the measured water. Bring to a boil, then cover the pan with a lid and cook for 20 minutes, until the vegetables are cooked.

Stir the salt and Pav Bhaji Masala into the pan and cook for 2 minutes, until well combined. Now stir in the grated potatoes and the remaining 350ml (12fl oz) measured water and cook for 10–12 minutes, until everything is cooked through.

Use a potato masher to mash the whole mixture while it is still in the pan, then cook for a final 2 minutes. Sprinkle over the coriander and as much extra butter as you would like and keep hot.

To serve, melt 1 tablespoon of the butter in a frying pan over medium heat. Put the 2 halves of 1 bread roll into the pan. Cook for 1 minute on each side, then remove from the pan. Repeat with the remaining rolls and butter. Serve the rolls with the piping-hot bhaji and lime wedges for squeezing over.

MOONG BEAN
SPECIAL

This recipe is based on a Mumbai dish known as matki special, an unusual combination of dal and potatoes prepared on the streets in massive pans under plastic shelters. Even in heavy rains, the people making it still seem to enjoy the cooking. In Mumbai I ate it with bread rolls, but it's also great with rice or roti. My version features dried mung beans because they are easier to find in the UK than the specific variety of green lentils used in India.

250g (9oz) mung beans
   (moong sabut)
1 litre (1³/4 pints) water
1¹/2 teaspoons salt
1 tablespoon sunflower oil
6 curry leaves
1 small green chilli, finely chopped
1 onion, finely chopped
3 garlic cloves, finely chopped
1cm (¹/2 inch) piece of fresh
   root ginger, peeled and
   finely chopped
1 teaspoon ground cumin
1 teaspoon ground coriander
¹/2 teaspoon chilli powder
1 tomato, finely chopped
1 floury potato, peeled and diced
150ml (¹/4 pint) boiling water
1 tablespoon lemon juice
bread or rice, to serve (optional)

Put the mung beans into a saucepan with the measured water and 1 teaspoon of the salt. Bring to the boil, partially cover the pan with a lid and cook over medium-low heat for 35–40 minutes, or until tender.

Heat the oil in a large saucepan set over medium heat. Add the curry leaves and green chilli and fry for a few seconds, then add the onion and cook for about 8–10 minutes, until golden brown, stirring occasionally.

Add the garlic and ginger and cook for 1 minute, then add the spices and remaining salt. Mix well, then add the tomato, potato and measured boiling water and mix again. Cover the pan with a lid and cook for 10 minutes, or until the potato is tender.

Tip the mung beans and their cooking liquid into the sauce and cook for a final 2 minutes, until well combined. Finish with the lemon juice and serve hot with bread or rice, if liked.

STICKY
BOMBAY CHICKEN

A friend took me to a street stall to try this sticky, spicy chicken. It's her favourite street snack and I love it too. The chicken could be cooked in a tandoor or an oven. Use wings instead of drumsticks if you prefer.

8 skinless chicken drumsticks
2 tablespoons dark soy sauce
1 tablespoon olive oil
20g (3/4oz) dark brown sugar
4 garlic cloves, finely chopped
2.5cm (1 inch) piece of fresh root ginger, peeled and finely chopped
1 red chilli, finely chopped
1 teaspoon five-spice powder
1 teaspoon salt
1 tablespoon toasted sesame seeds

Make a couple of slashes on each drumstick, ready for marinating.

Combine the soy sauce, olive oil, sugar, garlic, ginger, chilli, five-spice powder and salt in a large bowl. Mix well, then add the chicken and stir to coat. Leave to marinate for at least 1 hour or, preferably, cover the bowl with clingfilm and marinate overnight in the refrigerator.

Preheat the oven to 180°C (350°F), Gas Mark 4.

Tip the chicken and marinade into a shallow roasting tin and bake for 40 minutes, turning occasionally, until the chicken is cooked through. Sprinkle over the sesame seeds and serve hot.

Serves 4

VEGETABLE
PULAO

Made right in front of you on the streets of Mumbai,
this vegetarian pulao is super delicious. In Mumbai they
serve it with potato curry, green chutney and a little raita,
which is a great combination, but you can also enjoy
this satisfying rice dish on its own.

1 tablespoon sunflower oil
1 onion, finely chopped
6 spring onions, finely chopped
1 green pepper, finely chopped
2 tomatoes, finely chopped
150g (5¹/₂oz) fresh or frozen peas
1 teaspoon salt
1 teaspoon garam masala
¹/₂ teaspoon ground turmeric
¹/₄ teaspoon ground black pepper
4 servings of cooked basmati rice

Heat the oil in a saucepan over medium heat. Add the onion and cook for about 5 minutes, until softened. Reserve a handful of the green parts of the spring onion for garnish and add the rest to the onion in the pan. Cook for 2 minutes, until the spring onion begins to soften, then add the green pepper and tomatoes and mix well to combine.

If using frozen peas, blanch them in boiling water for 2 minutes and drain before use. Add the fresh or blanched frozen peas to the onion, mix well and cook for 2 minutes, until well combined, then stir in the salt, garam masala, turmeric and black pepper.

Stir the cooked rice into the saucepan and cook for a final 4–5 minutes, until the rice is heated through, then remove from the heat and serve hot.

POHA

Every corner of India has its own way of making this beloved breakfast dish, which means it tastes a little different everywhere you go. Poha is flattened or beaten rice, which has a lovely flakey texture when uncooked and becomes wonderfully soft once cooked. This dish is usually sold from small street stalls but can be found in restaurants too, and is sometimes accompanied by crispy snacks such as samosa and kachori.

2 tablespoons sunflower oil
1 teaspoon black mustard seeds
8 curry leaves
2 green chillies, halved lengthways
4 tablespoons roasted peanuts
1 onion, roughly chopped
1 floury potato, peeled and cut into 1cm (½ inch) dice
250g (9oz) flattened rice flakes (poha)
2 tablespoons yogurt
1 teaspoon salt
½ teaspoon ground turmeric
½ teaspoon chilli powder
2 tablespoons lemon juice
handful of coriander leaves, finely chopped
handful of gram flour noodles (sev)
lime wedges, to serve

Heat the oil in a wide saucepan over medium heat. Add the mustard seeds and, once they start to pop, stir in the curry leaves, green chillies, peanuts, onion and potato. Cover the pan with a lid and cook over low heat for about 10 minutes, until the potatoes are tender.

Meanwhile, put the flattened rice flakes in a sieve and rinse it with cold water, using just enough water to ensure all the flakes are wet. Tip it into a bowl and stir in the yogurt. Set aside for 5 minutes.

Return to the onion-potato mixture and add the salt, turmeric and chilli powder. Cook, stirring, for 1 minute, then add the yogurt-soaked rice flakes. Mix well and cook for 2 minutes, until well combined and the rice flakes are warmed through. Stir in the lemon juice.

Serve the poha hot in bowls, sprinkled with fresh chopped coriander and noodles, and accompanied by lime wedges for squeezing over.

EGG RICE

In Mumbai, as you pass street vendors selling egg rice you can see it being freshly prepared in big, flat tawa or cast iron skillets. This dish makes a great meal at any time of day and tastes brilliant with chilli chutney or ketchup. Making egg rice is a terrific way of using up leftover plain rice.

1 tablespoon sunflower oil
1 tablespoon salted butter
1 onion, finely chopped
1 small green chilli, finely chopped
1 tomato, finely chopped
1/2 teaspoon salt
1/4 teaspoon ground turmeric
1/4 teaspoon chilli powder
1/4 teaspoon garam masala
2 eggs
400g (14oz) cooked white rice

Heat the oil and butter in a large frying pan over medium heat. Add the onion and chilli and cook for about 5 minutes, until the onion begins to soften. Stir in the tomato and cook for 2 minutes, until the tomato has softened.

Use a potato masher to press the mixture a few times, then add the salt and spices and mix together well.

Break the eggs into the pan and stir quickly as though making scrambled eggs. Mash the mixture again a couple of times, then add the rice and mix thoroughly as it heats through and the egg cooks. Serve hot.

PURI ALU

This outstanding combination of comforting potato curry and deep-fried flatbread is very popular in North India and Mumbai. On special occasions people will cook it at home, too, as it is considered a festive dish. You can add green chutney and raita, if you like, or just eat it with some mango pickle.

For the potato curry
2 tablespoons sunflower oil
1 teaspoon black mustard seeds
6 curry leaves
2 garlic cloves, finely chopped
4 tomatoes, finely chopped
1 teaspoon salt
1 teaspoon garam masala
1 teaspoon ground coriander
1/2 teaspoon chilli powder
1/2 teaspoon ground turmeric
6 floury potatoes, boiled, peeled
  and roughly chopped
200ml (1/3 pint) water

For the puri
300g (10 1/2 oz) chapatti flour
160ml (5 1/2 fl oz) water
sunflower oil, for deep-frying

To make the potato curry, heat the oil in a saucepan over medium heat and add the mustard seeds. When they begin to pop, add the curry leaves and garlic and cook for 1 minute, until fragrant. Stir in the tomatoes, then cover the pan with a lid and cook for 6–8 minutes, until soft.

Stir the salt, garam masala, ground coriander, chilli powder and turmeric into the pan and cook for 1 minute, then add the chopped potatoes. Pour in the measured water and simmer for 10–15 minutes, stirring occasionally, until the gravy thickens slightly. Keep warm until ready to serve.

To make the puri dough, put the flour into a bowl and slowly add just enough of the measured water to form a dough that is soft rather than wet and tight. Put the dough into a bowl, cover the bowl with clingfilm and leave to rest for 10 minutes.

Divide the dough into 20 small balls and roll each portion into a 10cm (4 inch) circle.

Heat enough oil for deep-frying in a deep-fat fryer or heavy saucepan (ensuring the pan is no more than one-third full) to 180°C (350°F). Line a plate with some kitchen paper. Fry the puris, 1 at a time, for 1 minute on each side, until golden brown. Transfer to a paper-lined plate to drain excess oil. Serve the piping hot puris with the potato curry.

CORN ON THE COB
WITH LIME AND CHILLI

People love to eat this dish when the monsoon season hits
India and fresh corn becomes available. It sells so quickly
that street vendors make it even during the heavy rains.
Barbecuing over hot coals is easily the best and most delicious
way to cook fresh corn on the cob, and the simple flavourings
in this recipe really bring the corn to life.

3 corn cobs
3/4 teaspoon salt
3/4 teaspoon chilli powder
1 1/2 limes

Prepare a barbecue. Peel the husks and silks from the corn cobs and put the cobs on the hot barbecue. Cook, turning often, for about 5–10 minutes, depending on the heat of the barbecue, until golden and roasted all over. (Alternatively, cook the corn on the hob over a gas burner.)

Mix the salt and chilli together in a small bowl. Cut the lime in half and pat it, cut side-down, on the salt-chilli mixture.

Rub the crusted lime all over the cooked corn, squeezing the fruit as you do to give the corn a salty, sour and spicy flavour. Enjoy hot.

CHICKEN
FRIED RICE

This is a simple recipe for a dish that's made in minutes and tastes amazing. Enjoy it piping hot on its own or, as popularly served in India, with Manchurian or chilli chicken. To make it vegetarian, simply replace the chicken with vegetables.

2 tablespoons vegetable oil
2 garlic cloves, finely chopped
2.5cm (1 inch) piece of fresh root ginger, peeled and finely chopped
1 small green chilli, finely chopped
10 spring onions, chopped
200g (7oz) chicken breast, cut into 1cm (1/2 inch) pieces
1 tablespoon soy sauce
1 teaspoon salt
1 teaspoon rice wine vinegar
1 teaspoon chilli-garlic sauce
300g (10 1/2 oz) cooked basmati rice
2 eggs, lightly beaten

Heat the oil in a saucepan over medium heat. Add the garlic, ginger and chilli and cook for 1 minute, until softened. Set aside a handful of the green parts of the spring onions for garnish, then add the remainder to the pan and cook for 2 minutes, until softened or beginning to change colour.

Add the chicken pieces to the saucepan and stir-fry for 5 minutes, until the chicken is cooked through.

Stir in the soy sauce, salt, vinegar and chilli-garlic sauce, then add the cooked rice to the pan.

Slowly pour in the beaten egg, mixing really well. Cook for 2 minutes, until the egg is cooked, then sprinkle with the reserved spring onion and serve hot.

SICHUAN
CHICKEN

If you have read the recipe for Sichuan Sauce you will know that this is one fiery little dish! Simply add more sauce if you want it even spicier. This is best served with rice or noodles.

1 tablespoon sunflower oil
2.5cm (1 inch) piece of fresh root ginger, peeled and finely chopped
10 spring onions, finely chopped
6 tablespoons Sichuan Sauce (see page 224), plus extra as desired
1 teaspoon salt
1/2 teaspoon white pepper
500g (1lb 2oz) skinless chicken breast fillets, cut into small pieces
1 green pepper, thinly sliced
200ml (1/3 pint) boiling water
1 tablespoon cornflour
1 tablespoon cold water

Heat the oil in a large saucepan over medium heat. Add the ginger and cook for 1 minute, until fragrant, then add the spring onions, reserving a few of the green parts for garnish. Sauté for 2 minutes, until the spring onions begin to soften, then stir in the Sichuan Sauce, salt and white pepper.

Add the chicken pieces to the saucepan, stir well and cook for 5–7 minutes or until the chicken is almost done. Add the green pepper and cook for another minute. Pour in the measured boiling water and mix well.

In a small bowl, mix the cornflour with the measured cold water to make a paste. Stir this into the chicken and cook over high heat for 2 minutes or until the sauce thickens. Sprinkle over the reserved spring onions and serve hot.

VEGETABLE

MANCHURIAN

As with everywhere else, Chinese cuisine is big in India, and an important part of the street food scene, especially in Mumbai, where you will find the same three or four Chinese dishes served on every street. This vegetarian dish is very popular and mostly eaten with fried rice or noodles.

fried rice or noodles, to serve (optional)

For the vegetable balls
1/2 small cabbage, grated
1 carrot, grated
100g (3 1/2 oz) fine green beans, finely chopped
2 green chillies, finely chopped
100g (3 1/2 oz) plain flour
1 teaspoon salt
2 tablespoons cornflour
sunflower oil, for deep-frying

For the sauce
1 tablespoon sunflower oil
1 green chilli, finely chopped
2 garlic cloves, finely chopped
2.5cm (1 inch) piece of fresh root ginger, peeled and finely chopped
2 celery sticks, finely chopped
1 tablespoon soy sauce
1 teaspoon rice vinegar
1/2 teaspoon salt
700ml (1 1/4 pints) vegetable stock
2 tablespoons cornflour
1 tablespoon water

Combine all the ingredients for the vegetable balls, except the oil, in a large bowl. Mix well, then start pressing the ingredients together so that they cohere. Shape the mixture into balls the size of a lime – you should have around 24.

Heat enough oil for deep-frying in a deep-fat fryer or heavy saucepan (ensuring the pan is no more than one-third full) to 180°C (350°F). Line a plate with some kitchen paper. Add the vegetable balls to the hot oil and deep-fry for 2 minutes on each side or until golden brown. Transfer to the paper-lined plate to drain excess oil.

To make the sauce, heat the oil in a wide saucepan over medium heat and add the chilli, garlic, ginger and celery. Cook for 5 minutes, until the celery has softened. Add the soy sauce, vinegar and salt, then pour in the vegetable stock and bring the mixture to a boil.

Put the cornflour into a small bowl and mix in the measured water to make a smooth paste. Slowly stir this paste into the sauce and cook over high heat for 2 minutes, until the sauce has thickened slightly.

Pop the vegetable balls into the sauce and leave them to steep for 5 minutes, to heat through. Serve with rice or noodles, if liked.

MANCHURIAN CHAAT

I came across this amazing little dish in Mumbai recently and really enjoyed it. I've always loved Vegetable Manchurian (*see* page 155) but seeing it in chaat is unusual. This dish is spicy and crisp and makes a great snack or starter.

2 tablespoons sunflower oil
10 spring onions, finely chopped
3 tablespoons Sichuan Sauce
   (*see* page 224)
3 tablespoons tomato ketchup
1/2 teaspoon salt
24 Vegetable Manchurian balls
   (*see* page 155)

For the noodles
sunflower oil, for deep-frying
200g (7oz) egg noodles

To prepare the noodles, fill a deep-fat fryer or heavy pan with enough sunflower oil for deep-frying (ensuring the pan is no more than one-third full) and heat it to 190°C (375°F). Line a plate with some kitchen paper. When the oil is hot, add the noodles and fry for about 2 minutes, until golden brown. Transfer to the paper-lined plate to drain excess oil and cool. Once cool, wrap them in more kitchen paper and use a rolling pin to bash them into small pieces.

Heat the sunflower oil in a separate pan set over medium heat. Add the spring onions and fry for about 2 minutes, until they begin to soften. Stir in the Sichuan Sauce, ketchup and salt, then add the crispy noodles and mix well.

Cut the Vegetable Manchurian balls in half and pop them into the spicy mixture. Stir to combine, allow the balls to heat through, then serve hot.

FALOODA

Unusual but tasty, this sundae-meets-milkshake treat
is an amazing combination of flavours and textures.
Although falooda is found all over the country, I think the
best version comes from Mumbai. Sweet basil seeds and glass
noodles (falooda sev) can be tricky to source but you should
be able to find them online – it will be worth it in the end,
as this is a very special dessert. *See* photograph, page 159.

1 tablespoon sweet basil seeds
(sabja seeds)
500ml (18 fl oz) water
50g (1³/₄oz) glass noodles
(falooda sev)
8 tablespoons rose syrup
400ml (14fl oz) chilled milk
4 scoops of vanilla ice cream
handful of pistachio nuts,
finely chopped
handful of almonds, finely
chopped

Soak the basil seeds in
the measured water for
30 minutes. Meanwhile, cook
the noodles according to the
packet instructions and leave
to cool completely.

To assemble the falooda,
pour 2 tablespoons of the
rose syrup into a serving
glass. Add 2 tablespoons of
the now much expanded
soaked basil seeds, then 100ml
(3¹/₂fl oz) of the chilled milk.
Add a handful of noodles and
top with a scoop of ice cream.
Sprinkle over pistachios and
almonds. Repeat with the
remaining ingredients to
create 4 servings and serve
immediately.

CHOCOLATE

TOASTED SANDWICH

Cream cheese and chocolate taste heavenly when toasted together. This modern addition to Mumbai's street food scene is somewhat indulgent but a total treat. I tasted it on a recent trip to the city and loved it.

9 slices of white bread
unsalted butter, softened
150g (5½oz) cream cheese
300g (10½oz) ready-made
   chocolate sauce

Preheat a sandwich toaster.

Butter both sides of 2 slices of bread and place 1 of them in the hot sandwich toaster. Spread one-third of the cream cheese on that slice.

Take a third slice of the bread and spread chocolate sauce on 1 side. Fold it diagonally in half to make a triangle with the chocolate sauce on the inside. Place it on top of the cheese-covered slice in the sandwich toaster. Spread some more chocolate sauce on top and cover with the remaining buttered slice of bread.

Close the sandwich toaster and toast for 2 minutes or until golden brown all over.

Remove the toasted sandwich from the machine and repeat the process with the remaining sandwich ingredients to make 3 sandwiches.

Drizzle the last of the chocolate sauce on top of each toasted sandwich and serve.

NIMBU PAANI

Like a rose-scented lemonade, this is one of those refreshing drinks found on every corner of every street in India during the summer. The black salt adds a lovely spicy sourness to the taste of the citrus fruits.

125ml (4fl oz) lemon juice
juice of 2 limes
4 tablespoons icing sugar
1/2 teaspoon salt
1/2 teaspoon black salt
8 drops of rose water
800ml (1 1/3 pints) cold water
few ice cubes, to serve

Combine the citrus juices in a jug. Add the icing sugar, salts and rose water and mix until the sugar has dissolved. Stir in the measured water.

Put some ice into 4 glasses, pour over the nimbu paani and serve.

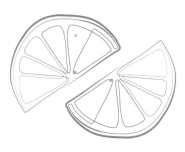

BHAKARWADI

These tiny sweet-savoury snacks are found at most of the tea stalls in Mumbai. The pastry is filled with beautiful spices and fried to give a crisp finish. Stored in an airtight box, they will keep you going for days – that is, if they last that long!

sunflower oil, for deep-frying

For the pastry
150g (5¹/₂oz) plain flour
50g (1³/₄oz) gram (chickpea) flour
¹/₄ teaspoon salt
¹/₄ teaspoon ground turmeric
about 100ml (3¹/₂fl oz) water

For the filling
25g (1oz) sesame seeds
25g (1oz) white poppy seeds
25g (1oz) desiccated coconut
1 teaspoon fennel seeds
1 teaspoon sunflower oil
1 teaspoon finely chopped ginger
1 tablespoon gram (chickpea) flour
¹/₂ teaspoon salt
¹/₂ teaspoon chilli powder
1¹/₂ teaspoon granulated sugar
1 teaspoon ground coriander
1 teaspoon ground cumin

To make the pastry, put the flours in a bowl with the salt and turmeric. Slowly mix in just enough of the measured water (or a little more, if necessary) to form a soft dough. Knead for 2 minutes, then cover the bowl with clingfilm and leave to rest for 15–20 minutes.

To make the filling, toast the sesame seeds in a dry pan over low heat for 2 minutes, without letting them change colour. Tip the seeds into a bowl. Repeat with the poppy seeds, then with the coconut, then the fennel seeds. Add the remaining filling ingredients to the seeds and coconut and mix well.

Divide the dough into 4 portions. Working with each portion in turn, roll it out into a thin circle with a diameter of roughly 22–23cm (8¹/₂–9 inches). Using a pastry brush, dampen the pastry circle with water. Sprinkle a quarter of the filling mixture over it and press down slightly. Roll up the circle like a Swiss roll, then cut crossways into pieces with a thickness of about 15mm (⁵/₈ inch).

Fill a deep-fat fryer or heavy saucepan with enough oil for deep-frying (ensuring the pan is no more than one-third full) and heat it to 170–180°C (340–350°F). Line a plate with some kitchen paper. Working in batches, fry the bhakarwadi for about 2 minutes on each side, until golden brown. Transfer to the paper-lined plate to drain excess oil. Serve hot or cold.

DELHI

Delhi is a sprawling city of contrasts. New Delhi, India's capital, is all tall buildings and huge malls, while to its north the Old City is a warren of narrow market lanes, full of tempting shops, bustle and madness. The glitter in the fabrics on sale is matched by flair in the local cuisine.

Some parts of New Delhi have completely lost touch when it comes to street food. It is to the Old City that you must head for the gems. There, you'll find stalls gathered around the shopping areas, outside stations and temples, and in popular recreation areas.

The markets host many long-established and famous stalls, which sell everything from light snacks and lassi to heavy meals. The spice markets have rows upon rows of shops, all with beautiful displays of familiar and exotic spices. And, of course, the fragrance as you walk through the bazaar is amazing.

Delhi's cuisine is well loved in other cities, especially the bhel and pav bhaji that can be enjoyed at any time of day. Delhi undoubtedly has the best chaat, whether that be aloo tikki, samosa or kachori. And Chinese flavours go down well in Delhi, too.

Indian people tend to be big foodies, but even by those standards, Delhi's residents love their food. And the more ghee or deep-frying there is involved, the better! Rich dishes such as chole bhature, puri alu and the many stuffed parathas are always popular, whether the weather is boiling hot or freezing cold.

This is the food I grew up with and adore to this day. In fact, my kids have become very fond of it too.

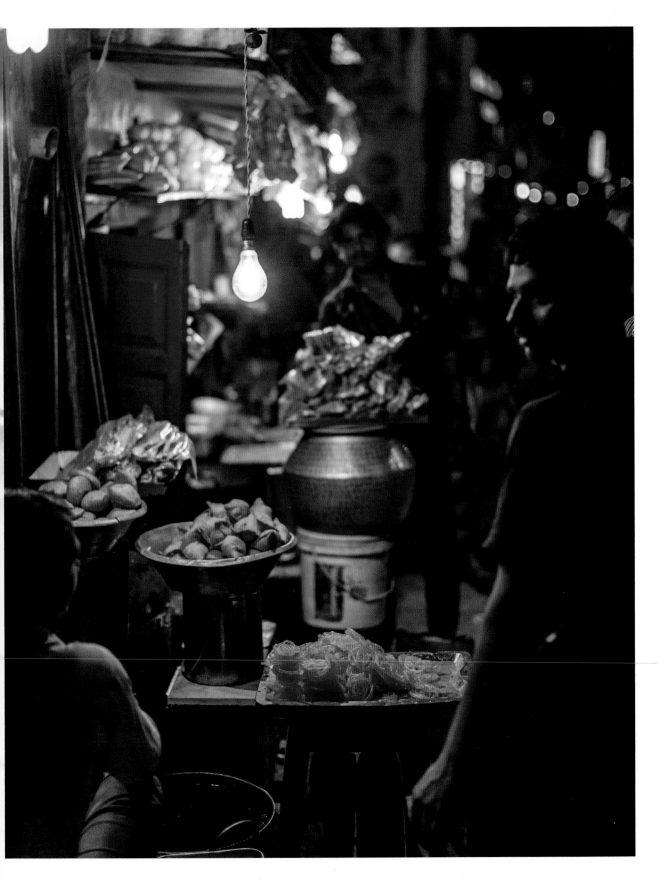

RAGDA PATTICE

Also known as alu tikki chaat, this scrumptious dish is found most often on the streets of Delhi and Mumbai. The potato cakes are made fresh in massive pans, deep-fried in ghee and then served with chickpeas or whole beans and chutney. With this recipe, I'm aiming for a healthier version that doesn't compromise on flavour.

For the chickpeas
1 tablespoon sunflower oil
1 teaspoon black mustard seeds
pinch of asafoetida
1/2 teaspoon salt
1/2 teaspoon Chaat Masala
  (see page 230)
1/2 teaspoon ground turmeric
2 x 400g (14oz) cans chickpeas

For the potato cakes
3 floury potatoes, boiled and
  peeled
1/2 teaspoon salt
1/4 teaspoon ground turmeric
1/4 teaspoon chilli powder
1 tablespoon ghee or sunflower oil

To serve
4 tablespoons Tamarind Chutney
  (see page 220)
handful of fine gram flour noodles
  (sev)

To prepare the chickpeas, heat the oil in a saucepan over medium heat and add the mustard seeds. Once they begin to pop, add the asafoetida then, after a few seconds, add the salt, Chaat Masala and turmeric and mix well. Add the chickpeas along with their canning liquid and simmer over high heat for 10–15 minutes, until very little liquid is left in the pan.

To make the potato cakes, mash the cooked potatoes until smooth, then add the salt, turmeric and chilli powder and mix well. Divide the mixture into 8 equal portions and shape them into patties.

Heat the ghee or sunflower oil in a frying pan over medium heat. Cook the potato cakes for about 3–4 minutes on each side, until they are golden brown and crispy.

Place 2 potato cakes on each serving plate and add 4 tablespoons of the chickpea mixture. Drizzle each portion with a tablespoon of Tamarind Chutney and finish with a sprinkling of noodles. Serve immediately.

Serves 4

SPROUTED
DAL CHAAT

Unlike a lot of street food, this dish is very healthy
and refreshing, and the only cooking required is boiling the
potato. I first tried it in Delhi and loved the idea that chaat
could be so nutritious. Start three days in advance of serving,
as the mung beans need time to soak and sprout.

100g (3½oz) mung beans
   (moong sabat)
250ml (9fl oz) water
1 small onion, finely chopped
1 tomato, deseeded and finely
   chopped
1 small floury potato, boiled,
   peeled and finely chopped
1 small green chilli, finely chopped
handful of fresh coriander leaves,
   finely chopped
½ teaspoon Chaat Masala
   (see page 230)
¼ teaspoon salt
juice of 1 lime

Soak the mung beans
overnight in the measured
water. On the next day, drain
the beans in a sieve and rinse
with fresh water, then put them
into a covered container, close
the container with a lid and
leave in a corner of the kitchen.

On the next day, repeat the
rinsing process, then return
the beans to the container,
cover with a lid and set aside
until the next day.

By this time, the beans should
have sprouted and developed
a soft crunch when eaten. Put
the sprouts into a bowl with
the remaining ingredients and
mix well. Serve immediately.

MASALA
PAPADS

Crisp and refreshing, this snack can be made in minutes and is also fairly healthy. This cucumber and tomato topping is lovely, but try it with other toppings, too, such as spring onions, spicy scrambled eggs, pickles and anything from the chutney section in this book. Papads, or poppadums as they are often called in the UK, are made from many different types of flour, as you will see from the wide range available in Asian stores. Feel free to use ready-cooked ones from supermarkets, too.

2 papads (poppadums)
sunflower oil, for shallow-frying
(optional)
2 handfuls of finely chopped
deseeded cucumber
2 handfuls of finely chopped
deseeded tomato
1 small green chilli, finely chopped
few coriander leaves, finely chopped
pinch of Chaat Masala
(see page 230)
2 tablespoons lemon juice
salt

Prepare the papads as you prefer. To shallow fry them, fill a frying pan with oil to a depth of about 2.5cm (1 inch) and set it over medium heat. Line a plate with some kitchen paper. When the oil is almost at smoking point, put 1 of the papads into the pan and cook it until it puffs up – this will take literally seconds. Remove it promptly, transfer it to the paper-lined plate and leave to drain while you fry the second papad. Alternatively, to toast the papads on the gas burner, hold each one with flameproof tongs and move it backwards and forwards over medium heat for about 1 minute on each side, until the papad curls and changes colour.

Put a handful of cucumber on each papad and follow with the tomato. Sprinkle with salt, then scatter over the green chilli and coriander leaves. Dust with Chaat Masala and squeeze over a little lemon juice to finish. Serve immediately.

PEA-STUFFED
PARATHA

Delhi is famous for its delicious stuffed paratha, which are made with all sorts of vegetables inside, as well as for sweet ones. These delicious paratha are made to order on the streets of Delhi, where they are deep-fried to make them extra tasty. I use just a little oil, which means you can enjoy them more often without feeling guilty. *See* photograph, pages 178–179.

ghee or sunflower oil, for frying

For the dough
300g (10½oz) chapatti flour, plus extra for dusting
¼ teaspoon salt
1 tablespoon sunflower oil
about 160ml (5½fl oz) water

For the filling
400g (14oz) frozen peas
1½ teaspoons salt
1 teaspoon cumin seeds
½ teaspoon chilli powder
1 teaspoon mango powder (amchur)

To serve
butter
chutney of your choice

To make the dough, put the flour, salt and oil in a bowl. Slowly add just enough of the measured water (or a little more, if necessary) to form a dough. Knead it for 2 minutes, then cover the bowl with clingfilm and leave to rest for 15 minutes.

To make the filling, boil the peas in a small saucepan for about 5–7 minutes, until tender. Drain the peas and leave to cool slightly.

Put the boiled peas into a bowl with the remaining filling ingredients and mix well. Use a masher to press it a few times, ensuring all the spices are mixed well with the peas. Divide the mixture into 8 portions.

Divide the dough into 8 even portions, too. Roll out each piece of dough on a lightly floured surface into a circle with a diameter of about 7.5cm (3 inches).

Spoon 1 portion of the pea mixture onto the centre of each dough circle and fold the dough over to enclose the filling. Press it with your fingertips and roll it out again so that it measures roughly 15cm (6 inches) in diameter.

Heat a frying pan over medium heat and cook each paratha for 2 minutes on each side, until beginning to colour. Drizzle up to 1 teaspoon ghee or sunflower oil over the paratha and continue to cook for about 1–2 minutes, until golden brown.

Serve hot with butter and a chutney of your choice.

PANEER-STUFFED
PARATHA

Paratha can be made in many different ways. Here I am sharing one of my favourite fillings – a spicy cheese and onion mixture, which goes well with any chutney. *See* photograph, pages 178–179.

ghee or sunflower oil, for frying

For the dough
300g (10¹/₂oz) chapatti flour, plus extra for dusting
¹/₄ teaspoon salt
1 tablespoon sunflower oil
about 160ml (5¹/₂fl oz) water

For the filling
225g (8oz) paneer, grated
1 onion, finely chopped
1 green chilli, finely chopped
¹/₂ teaspoon salt
¹/₂ teaspoon chilli powder
¹/₂ teaspoon garam masala
1 teaspoon black mustard seeds
handful of fresh coriander leaves, finely chopped

To serve
butter
chutney of your choice

To make the dough, put the flour, salt and oil in a bowl. Slowly mix in just enough of the measured water (or a little more, if necessary) to form a dough.

Turn out the dough onto a lighty floured work surface and knead for 2 minutes, then put the dough into a bowl, cover the bowl with clingfilm and leave to rest for 15 minutes.

To make the filling, combine all the ingredients in a bowl and mix thoroughly. Divide roughly into 8 portions.

Divide the dough into 8 portions too. Roll out each piece of dough on a lightly floured surface into a circle with a diameter of about 7.5cm (3 inches).

Place 1 paneer portion in the centre of each dough circle and fold the dough over to enclose the filling. Press it with your fingertips to seal and roll out again on a lightly floured surface into a circle that measures roughly 15cm (6 inches) in diameter.

Heat a frying pan over medium heat and cook each paratha for 2 minutes on each side, until beginning to colour. Drizzle up to 1 teaspoon ghee or sunflower oil over the paratha and continue to cook for about 1–2 minutes, until golden brown.

Serve hot with butter and a chutney of your choice.

STUFFED
ALU TIKKI

Crispy on the outside and very spicy inside, these delicious potato croquettes are filled with spiced lentils and eaten with Tamarind Chutney, and are extremely popular on the streets of North India.

Tamarind Chutney (*see* page 220), to serve

For the stuffing
100g (3½oz) split yellow lentils (moong dal)
¼ teaspoon salt
pinch of ground turmeric
200ml (⅓ pint) water
1 teaspoon sunflower oil
pinch of asafoetida
1 green chilli, finely chopped
½ teaspoon ground cumin
½ teaspoon mango powder (amchur)
handful of fresh coriander leaves, finely chopped

For the tikki
4 floury potatoes, boiled and peeled
½ teaspoon salt
¼ teaspoon chilli powder
sunflower oil, for shallow-frying

To make the stuffing, put the lentils, salt and turmeric into a saucepan with the measured water and leave to soak for 1 hour.

Once the soaking time has elapsed, bring the mixture to a boil, then simmer for 10–12 minutes, until all the water has evaporated and the lentils are half cooked.

In a separate saucepan, heat the oil over medium heat. Add the asafoetida and cook for just a few seconds, then add the green chilli, followed by the ground cumin and mango powder. Mix well, then add the parcooked lentils and coriander leaves and mix again. Cook for 1 minute or so, until the mixture is nice and dry. Set aside to cool completely.

To make the tikki, mash the cooked potatoes in a bowl until smooth. Add the salt and chilli powder and mix well. Divide the mixture into 8 portions. Take 1 portion in the palm of your hand and roll it into a ball. Make a hole in the centre by pressing your thumb into it, then press out the hole to make it slightly larger. Stuff it with 1 tablespoon of the lentil mixture, then smooth the mashed potato around it to return it to a ball shape and to seal it well. Repeat with the remaining portions of potato mixture and the filling.

Heat enough sunflower oil for shallow-frying in a frying pan over medium heat. Line a plate with some kitchen paper. Fry the tikkis a few at a time for 2–3 minutes on each side, until crisp and golden brown. Transfer to the paper-lined plate to drain excess oil. Enjoy them hot with Tamarind Chutney.

PANI PURI

This is my all-time favourite street food. Pani puri, also known as gol gappa and puchka, consists of crisp puffed puri that are filled with a spicy-sour water and delectably spiced potato. There are many interesting ways of making them in India. This variation is super delicious and very moreish. *See* photograph, page 183.

For the puri
100g (3½oz) plain flour
100g (3½oz) semolina
½ teaspoon salt
about 6 tablespoons water
sunflower oil, for deep-frying

For the spicy water
50g (1¾oz) mint leaves
10g (¼oz) fresh coriander leaves
1 small green chilli
1 tablespoon lime juice
1 teaspoon tamarind paste
1 teaspoon toasted cumin seeds
2 teaspoons granulated sugar
1½ teaspoons salt
500ml (18fl oz) water
few ice cubes

For the filling
1 large floury potato, boiled
  and peeled
¼ teaspoon salt
¼ teaspoon chilli powder

To make the puri, mix the flour, semolina and salt in a bowl. Mix in just enough of the measured water (or a little more, if necessary) to form a soft dough, adding it 1 tablespoon at a time. Cover the bowl with clingfilm and leave to rest for 30 minutes.

After the resting time has elapsed, pinch the dough into pieces about the size of hazelnuts. Roll out each piece into a very thin circle with a diameter of about 2cm (¾ inch). As you work, keep the rest of the dough covered with a clean tea towel so that it does not dry out.

Fill a deep-fat fryer or heavy saucepan with enough oil for deep-frying (ensuring the pan is no more than one-third full) and heat it to 190°C (375°F). Line a plate with some kitchen paper. Fry the puri a few at a time for 1–2 minutes on each side, until golden brown. Transfer to the paper-lined plate to drain excess oil.

To make the spicy water, put all the ingredients except the water and ice cubes into a food processor and blend them to a smooth paste. Transfer to a jug, add the measured water and mix well.

To make the filling, put the potato into a bowl and finely chop or mash it, then mix in the salt and chilli powder.

Just before you are ready to serve, add the ice cubes to the spicy water.

Taking 1 puri at a time, make a little hole in the top with your thumb and fill the puri with a small amount of the potato mixture. Pour in some spicy water and serve immediately.

MASALA CHANA CHAAT

This recipe is inspired by a sour, fresh-tasting masala chana chaat I enjoyed from a street stall in Delhi. The stallholder had boiled the chickpeas beforehand and was making the chaat fresh. It is so easy and quick to do, and makes a perfect starter or light meal, but is also very good with any barbecue or roast.

2 tablespoons sunflower oil
1 large onion, finely chopped
1 green chilli, finely chopped
2 tomatoes, finely chopped
1 teaspoon Chaat Masala
  (see page 230)
1/2 teaspoon chilli powder
1/2 teaspoon salt
400g (14oz) can chickpeas, drained
  and rinsed
1 tablespoon lime juice
handful of fresh coriander leaves,
  finely chopped
handful of dill, finely chopped

Heat the oil in a wide saucepan. Add the chopped onion and green chilli and cook over medium heat for 2 minutes, until softened.

Add the tomatoes and cook for just 1 minute, then stir in the Chaat Masala, chilli powder, salt and chickpeas and mix well.

Take the pan off the heat and stir in the lime juice and fresh herbs. Enjoy hot or cold.

BHATURA

Traditionally, this deep-fried flatbread is served with Chole, a well-known chickpea dish. It's a wonderfully comforting combination in cold weather and, although very popular on the streets, especially in North India, it's almost invariably served at weddings too. *See* photograph, page 186.

300g (10½oz) plain flour
¼ teaspoon baking powder
¼ teaspoon salt
3 tablespoons yogurt
about 120ml (4fl oz) water
sunflower oil, for deep-frying
Chole (see page 187) or a curry
  of your choice, to serve

Combine the flour, baking powder, salt and yogurt in a bowl and mix well. Slowly add just enough of the measured water to form a soft (but not wet) dough. Knead the dough on a clean work surface for 2 minutes, or until smooth. Put the dough into a bowl, cover the bowl with clingfilm and leave to rest for 15 minutes.

Once the resting time has elapsed, divide the dough into 8 portions if making large bhatura, or 10–12 if making smaller ones.

Heat enough oil for deep-frying in a deep-fat fryer or heavy saucepan (ensuring the pan is no more than one-third full) to 180°C (350°F). Line a plate with some kitchen paper.

Working with 1 portion of dough at a time, roll out each portion into a circle with a diameter of around 17–20cm (6½–8 inches) for large bhatura, or 10–13cm (4–5 inches) for small ones. Fry them for about 1 minute on each side, until lightly golden. Transfer to the paper-lined plate to drain excess oil.

Serve hot with Chole or any other curry.

CHOLE

One of the ultimate curries of the North, this chickpea curry is often paired with Bhatura, a deep-fried flatbread sold piping hot originally on the streets of Delhi but, now, all over the country. This combination should be on everyone's must-try list when visiting India. You can keep it light by eating this curry with rice or chapatti, if preferred.

3 tablespoons sunflower oil
2 black cardamom pods
2 green cardamom pods
4 cloves
1 cinnamon stick
2 bay leaves
1 teaspoon cumin seeds
2 large onions, grated or blitzed to a paste in a food processor
3 garlic cloves, finely chopped
2.5cm (1 inch) piece of fresh root ginger, peeled and finely chopped
2 tomatoes, grated
200ml (1/3 pint) water
1 1/2 teaspoons salt
1 teaspoon ground turmeric
1 teaspoon chilli powder, plus extra to garnish
1 teaspoon mango powder (amchur)
1 tablespoon ground coriander
1 tablespoon garam masala
2 x 400g (14oz) cans chickpeas
handful of fresh coriander leaves, finely chopped
sliced onion, to garnish
Bhatura (see page 185), to serve

Heat the oil in a wide saucepan and add the black and green cardamom pods, cloves, cinnamon and bay leaves and cook for 1 minute, until they begin to change colour. Add the cumin and, once it starts to sizzle, add the onion. Cook over low to medium heat, stirring often, for about 10–15 minutes, until the onion is dark golden brown.

Stir the garlic and ginger into the saucepan and cook for 1 minute. Then stir in the tomatoes and 100ml (3 1/2fl oz) of the measured water, cover the pan with a lid and cook over low heat for 20 minutes, until the tomatoes are soft and the mixture comes together as a sauce. Add the salt and spices and mix well.

Now add the chickpeas with their canning liquid and the remaining 100ml (3 1/2fl oz) water. Bring the mixture to a boil, then cover the pan with a lid and simmer for 20 minutes, until the chickpeas are soft. Use a masher to crush just a few of the chickpeas so that they break down and thicken the sauce. Sprinkle over the coriander leaves, garnish with the onion slices sprinkled with chilli powder, and serve with the Bhatura.

POTATO AND PEA
SAMOSAS

Samosas are perhaps the most popular Indian street food, known all over the world. The variety of fillings is endless. This classic potato and pea filling is my favourite.

sunflower oil, for deep-frying

For the pastry
200g (7oz) plain flour
1/2 teaspoon salt
1/2 teaspoon carom seeds
3 tablespoons sunflower oil, plus extra for greasing
about 5 tablespoons water

For the filling
1 tablespoon sunflower oil
1 teaspoon mustard seeds
1 green chilli, finely chopped
1 teaspoon salt
1/2 teaspoon chilli powder
1 teaspoon mango powder (amchur)
1/2 teaspoon garam masala
100g (3 1/2 oz) fresh or frozen peas
5 floury potatoes, boiled, peeled and mashed

To serve
Coriander and Spinach Chutney (see page 228)
Mint Chutney (see page 228)
Tamarind Chutney (see page 220)

To make the pastry, put the flour, salt and carom seeds in a bowl and add the sunflower oil. Use your fingers to rub the oil into the flour. Slowly add just enough of the measured water to form a dough. Knead for a few minutes, until smooth, then put the dough into an oiled bowl, cover the bowl with clingfilm and leave to rest for 15–20 minutes.

While the dough is resting, prepare the filling. Heat the oil in a saucepan over medium heat. Add the mustard seeds. Once they begin to pop, stir in the green chilli, salt and dry spices and mix well. Add the peas and cook for 5–6 minutes, until they begin to soften. Add the potato, mix well and cook for 2 minutes more, until well combined. Leave the mixture in the pan and set aside to cool.

Return to the samosa pastry and shape it into a long cylinder. Cut the cylinder into 12 equal portions. Roll out each portion into a circle with a diameter of 12–13cm (4 1/2 – 5 inches). Cut the circles in half.

Take 1 semicircle of pastry in the palm of your hand and brush some water along its straight edge. Shape it into a cone by folding it in half on the straight edge, then sticking the 2 straight edges together. Put 1 tablespoon of the potato mixture into the cone. Brush the open end of the pastry with water and press together to seal. Repeat with the remaining ingredients.

Heat enough oil for deep-frying in a deep-fat fryer or heavy saucepan (ensuring the pan is no more than one-third full) to 180°C (350°F). Fry the samosas 2 or 3 at a time for 2–3 minutes on each side, until golden and crispy.

Serve hot with the two green chutneys and some Tamarind Chutney.

BREAD
PAKORA

Although popular in all parts of India, bread pakoras are generally spicier in some regions than others. There are other subtle differences too – some people batter the bread on both sides while others batter just one side, and sometimes it is made into a sandwich. I have fond memories of enjoying these tasty pakoras piping hot with fresh green chutney on a lovely trip to Amritsar in North India.

sunflower oil, for deep-frying
4 slices of white bread
Coriander and Spinach Chutney (*see* page 228), to serve

For the potato mixture
1 teaspoon sunflower oil
1/2 teaspoon mustard seeds
1/2 teaspoon salt
1/4 teaspoon chilli powder
1/4 teaspoon ground turmeric
2 floury potatoes, boiled, peeled and mashed

For the batter
200g (7oz) gram (chickpea) flour
1 teaspoon salt
1/2 teaspoon chilli powder
1/2 teaspoon ground turmeric
1/2 teaspoon garam masala
about 400ml (14fl oz) water

Heat the oil for the potato mixture in a small frying pan over medium heat. Add the mustard seeds and, when they begin to pop, add the salt, chilli powder and turmeric and mix well. Stir in the mashed potatoes, cook for 2 minutes, then set aside to cool.

Heat enough oil for deep-frying in a deep-fat fryer or large saucepan (ensuring the pan is no more than one-third full) to 180°C (350°F). Line a plate with some kitchen paper.

Meanwhile, make the batter. Mix the gram flour, salt and spices in a bowl and slowly add just enough of the measured water to make a slightly runny batter – the consistency should be similar to that of crêpe batter.

Take a slice of bread and spread half the potato mixture on top of it. Sandwich with a second slice of bread and press together well. Repeat with the remaining bread and potato mixture and cut each sandwich into 4 triangles.

Once the oil is hot, dip the sandwich triangles in the batter and deep-fry for 3–4 minutes on each side, until golden brown. Transfer to the paper-lined plate to drain excess oil. (To make a healthier version, cook the sandwich triangles in a frying pan with very little oil.) Serve hot with green chutney.

DAHI VADA

Popular street food in **Delhi**, these lentil dumplings soaked in yogurt are also served as a side dish in **North Indian** meals to balance the hot, spicy curries. This recipe has very few ingredients, but the flavours work together beautifully.

Tamarind Chutney (see page 220), to serve

For the vada
200g (7oz) split black lentils (urad dal)
500ml (18fl oz) water
15mm (5/6 inch) piece of fresh root ginger, peeled and chopped
1/2 teaspoon salt
1 small green chilli, finely chopped
sunflower oil, for deep-frying

For the yogurt sauce
300ml (1/2 pint) natural yogurt
1/2 teaspoon salt
1/2 teaspoon ground cumin, plus extra to garnish (optional)
1/4 teaspoon chilli powder, plus extra to garnish (optional)
1/4 teaspoon sugar
5 tablespoons water

To make the vada, soak the lentils in the measured water overnight or for at least 4 hours.

Drain the soaked lentils, then use a food processor or blender to process the lentils, ginger, salt and chilli to a thick paste. Add a few drops of water to loosen the mixture if necessary, but no more as the paste needs to be thick.

Transfer the paste to a bowl and beat with a wooden spoon or whisk for 5–7 minutes, until the mixture is light and fluffy.

Fill a deep-fat fryer or a heavy saucepan with enough sunflower oil for deep-frying (ensuring the pan is no more than one-third full) and heat it to 170–180°C (340–350°F) but no higher, to allow the vada to cook through. Line a plate with some kitchen paper. Shape the mixture into portions roughly the size of small lemons.

Working in small batches, fry the vada a few at a time for 2–3 minutes, until light golden. Transfer to the paper-lined plate and leave to drain excess oil while you fry the remaining vada.

To make the yogurt sauce, combine all the ingredients in a bowl.

Soak each vada in a bowl of lukewarm water for 2 minutes. Press each of them between your palms to squeeze out excess water, then dip them in the yogurt sauce and place them on a shallow serving dish. Pour the remaining yogurt sauce over them. Sprinkle over a little extra cumin and chilli powder, if desired. Drizzle the Tamarind Chutney on top and chill until ready to serve.

TAWA PANEER

This is one of those dishes that keeps you going back for more.
I once had this served with freshly made naan in Delhi on a
late-night trip to the market with my sister. The taste has
stayed with me forever. Now my family adore it too –
it's their favourite paneer dish.

rice or naan bread, to serve
(optional)

For the marinated paneer
50ml (2fl oz) natural yogurt
1 tablespoon tomato purée
1/4 teaspoon salt
1/4 teaspoon ground turmeric
1/4 teaspoon chilli powder
225g (8oz) paneer, cut into dice
2 tablespoons sunflower oil

For the sauce
2 tablespoons sunflower oil
1/2 teaspoon cumin seeds
1/2 teaspoon carom seeds
2.5cm (1 inch) piece of fresh
root ginger, peeled and
finely chopped
2 garlic cloves, finely chopped
1 onion, finely chopped
1 green chilli, finely chopped
1 tablespoon tomato purée
1/2 teaspoon salt
1/2 teaspoon chilli powder
1/2 teaspoon ground coriander
1/2 teaspoon garam masala
200ml (1/3 pint) water
1 tablespoon kasuri methi
2 tablespoons double cream

To make the marinade, combine the yogurt, tomato purée, salt, turmeric and chilli powder in a bowl and mix well. Add the paneer and stir so that the cubes are well covered in the marinade. Cover the bowl with clingfilm and set aside for 1 hour.

Meanwhile, start making the sauce. Heat the sunflower oil in a wide saucepan set over medium heat. Add the cumin and carom seeds and cook until they begin to sizzle. Mix in the ginger and garlic and cook for 1 minute, then stir in the onion and chilli and cook, stirring occasionally, for about 8–10 minutes, until the onion turns golden brown.

Stir the tomato purée, salt, chilli powder, ground coriander, garam masala and measured water into the pan, then cover the pan with a lid, reduce the heat to low and cook for 10–15 minutes, until cooked through. Remove the pan from the heat and set aside.

To cook the paneer, heat the oil in a frying pan. Lift the cheese cubes from the marinade and fry in batches for about 2 minutes, turning to colour them evenly, until golden brown. As you finish each batch, transfer it to the sauce.

Once all the paneer is cooked and added to the sauce, put the sauce back on the hob over medium heat. Stir in the kasuri methi and double cream and cook for 5 minutes, until the cream has been heated. Serve hot with rice or naan, if liked.

MALPUA

Highly indulgent, this filling dish is not only super sweet but also very moreish. My mum would make malupa at home during monsoon season, to comfort us when it was raining outside. I also remember eating them at Indian weddings with a side of ice cream or rabdi (an Indian dessert made from condensed milk) – I'd always keep room for this dessert after the main meal! They are sold piping hot on the streets of Delhi and in many northern areas.

ice cream or whipped cream,
  to serve

For the malpua
150g (5½oz) plain flour
½ teaspoon ground cardamom
½ teaspoon baking powder
½ teaspoon toasted fennel seeds
200ml (⅓ pint) milk
50ml (2fl oz) water
sunflower oil, for deep-frying

For the syrup
400g (14oz) caster sugar
400ml (14fl oz) water

To make the malpua, combine the dry ingredients in a mixing bowl. Mix the milk and water in a jug. Slowly add just enough of the liquid to the dry ingredients, whisking well, to give a mixture the consistency of pancake batter.

Heat enough oil for deep-frying in a deep-fat fryer or heavy saucepan (ensuring the pan is no more than one-third full) to 180°C (350°F).

Meanwhile, make the syrup. Put the caster sugar and measured water into a saucepan and bring to a boil, then simmer for 7–8 minutes. Set aside while you fry the malpua.

Using a small serving spoon, put spoonfuls of the batter into the hot oil. (Work in batches if necessary to ensure you do not to overcrowd the pan.) Fry for 2 minutes on each side, until golden brown. Transfer the malpua to the sugar syrup to leave to soak for 5 minutes. Serve hot with ice cream or whipped cream.

JALEBI

I am a big fan of these syrup-soaked fritters and have tried them in every Indian city I have ever visited. The ones in Delhi were good, but the best have been in my hometown, Jabalpur, and in Amritsar in the north. This is a recipe for my own version, which is simple to make but does need a little time to prepare, as the batter needs to stand overnight. Jalebi are traditionally fried in ghee, which gives them an amazing flavour, but sometimes I use sunflower oil instead. They go really well with ice cream. *See* photograph, page 199.

100g (3½oz) plain flour, plus an extra 1 teaspoon for the following day
300ml (½ pint) water
200g (7oz) granulated sugar
10 cardamom pods
pinch of saffron
ghee or sunflower oil, for deep-frying
ice cream, to serve (optional)

Put the 100g (3½oz) of flour into a bowl with 100ml (3½fl oz) of the measured water and whisk for about 10 minutes. Cover the bowl with clingfilm and leave in a warm part of the kitchen overnight. On the next day, add the remaining flour, whisk well, then pour the batter into a squeezy bottle.

Put the sugar, cardamom and saffron in a saucepan with the remaining 200ml (⅓ pint) measured water. Heat gently over low heat until the sugar dissolves, then simmer for 6–8 minutes to make a syrup. Keep warm.

Fill a deep-fat fryer or heavy saucepan with enough oil for deep-frying (ensuring the pan is no more than one-third full). Heat the oil to 180°C (350°F). Working in batches, carefully pipe swirls of the batter into the hot fat and cook for about 2 minutes, until golden on each side. Remove the jalebi from the pan and immediately pop them into the syrup. Leave to soak for 3–4 minutes, then serve immediately, with ice cream, if desired.

PHIRNI

A staple of North Indian cuisine, this dessert is available
from street stalls during winter. It is similar to kheer
(Indian rice pudding) but phirni is made with rice paste and
set in clay pots, which enhances the flavour. Some of the
best phirni I have ever eaten has been in Delhi.

100g (3½oz) long-grain white rice
4 tablespoons water
1 litre (1¾ pints) milk
large pinch of saffron
1 teaspoon ground cardamom
100g (3½oz) golden caster sugar
handful of pistachio nuts,
   roughly chopped

Soak the rice in the measured water for 15 minutes, then use a blender or food processor to blend the rice and water to a coarse paste – you don't want it to be smooth.

Combine the milk and saffron in a heavy saucepan and bring to the boil. Add the rice paste and mix well. Reduce the heat to low and cook for 30–40 minutes, stirring every 5–7 minutes, until the rice is cooked. Add the cardamom and caster sugar and mix well.

Pour the phirni into clay pots if you have them, otherwise use ceramic or glass bowls. Sprinkle the pistachios on top and chill for a few hours before serving cold.

CARDAMOM AND
PISTACHIO KULFI

Kulfi (Indian ice cream) is particularly popular in Delhi, where you find an astonishing variety of flavours these days, from chocolate and mint to paan, yet the traditional combination of cardamom and pistachios remains my favourite. Making kulfi requires patience – no short cuts can give the same amount of flavour as hours spent reducing the milk, so it's definitely worth the effort.

1.5 litres (2¾ pints) milk
50g (1¾oz) golden caster sugar
½ teaspoon ground cardamom
3 tablespoons finely chopped pistachio nuts, plus extra to decorate

Pour the milk into a large, heavy-based saucepan. Bring it to the boil, then reduce the heat to low and simmer for 3 hours, stirring every 5–7 minutes to ensure the milk does not stick to the bottom of the pan.

Once the milk has reduced by two-thirds, measure it to ensure the volume has reduced to 500ml (18fl oz), then return it to the pan. Add the sugar and cardamom and stir for 1 minute, then add the pistachios. Pour the mixture into a jug and leave it to cool a little.

Divide the mixture between 6 kulfi cones (use plastic containers if you don't have any) and freeze overnight.

When ready to serve, dip the cones in warm water for a few seconds, then turn out the kulfi onto individual serving plates. Sprinkle with the extra pistachios to serve.

CHAAS

Chaas is a very refreshing drink; a lighter, savoury version of the popular yogurt-based drink lassi that is traditionally made with buttermilk. In India, it helps people to cope with the summer heat. It's made in homes as well as on the streets and, as with all street food, there are many ways of making it. Although lots of Delhi street stalls make great chaas, I'm sticking with my mum's recipe! She made butter and ghee at home and the buttermilk used for this was a by-product. Since I can't get that quality and taste of buttermilk here in the UK, I prefer using natural yogurt.

100ml (3½fl oz) natural yogurt
½ teaspoon salt
¼ teaspoon ground cumin
10 mint leaves
1 teaspoon finely chopped fresh root ginger
300ml (½ pint) water
few ice cubes, to serve (optional)

Put the yogurt into a bowl and whisk until smooth. Add the salt and cumin and mix well.

Bash the mint and ginger together using a pestle and mortar until smooth. Stir the paste into the yogurt.

Whisk the measured water into the yogurt so that all is well combined. Add ice to 2 glasses, if desired, pour over the chaas and serve.

CARROT
HALWA

People make this sweet, comforting pudding, known as gajar ka halwa, in winter, when carrots come into season. You'll find it in Delhi and throughout Northern India. People prepare it at home or buy it from street stalls, where the vendors keep the dish warm on large skillets. It is often made with khoya, a thickened milk, but below is a recipe for a slightly lighter version, made with regular milk.

2 tablespoons ghee
500g (1lb 2oz) carrots, peeled and grated
500ml (18fl oz) milk
50g (1¾oz) granulated sugar
½ teaspoon ground cardamom
25g (1oz) cashew nuts, roughly chopped
25g (1oz) almonds, roughly chopped, plus extra to decorate
raisins, to decorate

Heat the ghee in a wide saucepan over medium heat. Add the grated carrot and cook for 5 minutes, until it changes colour. Add the milk and bring to a boil. Once the mixture is bubbling, reduce the heat to very low and cook for 40–45 minutes, uncovered, stirring every 5 minutes, until all the milk is absorbed by the carrot.

Add the sugar and cardamom to the pan and cook for 5 minutes, until the sugar has melted. Stir in the cashews and almonds. Serve either hot or cold, with the almonds and raisins sprinkled on top.

KAJU KISHMISH
ICE CREAM

Cashew nut and raisin ice cream reminds me of a street-side ice cream stall my sisters and I used to visit with our dad as a special treat. Even today I still remember the flavours. The stall is not there anymore but I found a similar ice cream being sold at a street-side stall on my recent visit to Delhi and this recipe is as close as I could get to it.

4 egg yolks
50g (1³/₄oz) caster sugar
250ml (9fl oz) milk
125ml (4fl oz) double cream
1 teaspoon vanilla extract
30g (1oz) raisins, roughly chopped
30g (1oz) cashew nuts, finely chopped

Put the yolks and sugar into a heatproof bowl and whisk for 7–8 minutes until pale and fluffy. Set aside.

Heat the milk, cream and vanilla in a saucepan over low heat until the mixture just begins to bubble.

Slowly pour the hot milk mixture onto the yolks, whisking continuously. Tip the lot back into the saucepan and cook it over a low heat for 8–10 minutes, stirring continuously, to make a custard. Once the mixture thickens, remove the pan from the heat and leave to cool slightly.

Pour the custard into an ice cream maker and churn according to the manufacturer's instructions. Alternatively, transfer to a freezerproof container, freeze for 1 hour and stir hourly, returning to the freezer between each stir, until smooth. Just before the ice cream is ready, add the cashews and raisins.

Transfer the ice cream to a container and freeze until fully set.

SHAHI TUKDA

One of my childhood favourites, shahi tukda is a dessert
my mum would make at home on special occasions,
but it is also found on the streets of Delhi during winter.
The name translates to 'royal piece', which indicates
the beautiful richness of what is otherwise a fairly simple
combination of bread soaked in thick, scented milk
and topped with crunchy nuts.

500ml (18fl oz) milk
1/4 teaspoon ground cardamom
1/4 teaspoon rose water
100g (3¹/₂oz) condensed milk
4 slices of white bread
4 tablespoons ghee
handful of almonds, thinly sliced
handful of pistachio nuts,
  thinly sliced

Put the milk into a heavy
saucepan, bring it to a simmer
and cook over low heat for
about 1 hour, until it has
reduced to a quarter of its
original volume. Stir in the
cardamom powder, rose water
and condensed milk and
cook for 2 minutes, until well
combined. Set aside to cool.

Trim the crusts off the bread
and cut each slice diagonally
into 2 triangles. Heat a frying
pan over medium heat and
put 1 tablespoon ghee into it.
Add 2 triangles of bread and
cook for about 1–2 minutes on
each side, until golden brown.
Repeat with the remaining
ghee and bread.

Dip each piece of fried bread
into the cooled thick milk
for just a few seconds, then
transfer to a serving dish. Don't
leave the bread to steep in the
milk or it will disintegrate.

Once all the slices have been
soaked and arranged on the
dishes, pour the leftover milk
over the bread and sprinkle
the almonds and pistachios
on top. Serve warm or at
room temperature.

MANGO LASSI

I first had this delicious mango lassi in Delhi and, since then, have always made it at home during mango season. In India, lassi is considered a hot summer's drink as the ice and yogurt help you to cool down.

seeds from 5 green cardamom
  pods
200g (7oz) mango pulp
200ml (1/3 pint) natural yogurt
100ml (31/2fl oz) milk
1 tablespoon granulated sugar
few ice cubes

Using a pestle and mortar, grind the cardamom seeds to a powder.

Combine the mango pulp, yogurt, milk, sugar and ground cardamom in a blender. Add the ice cubes and blitz for 1 minute. Pour into 3 glasses and serve immediately.

MASALA CHAI

The backbone of Indian street food culture, this drink is available in every nook and cranny of almost every street in India. Everyone has their favourite chai stalls, which they'll visit daily, whether it's day or night. When I was in my final year of college and we were working late at night, a chai walla would come to the gate on a bicycle at around 1am with piping hot chai in a container. All the students who were still up would go and sit in a big group just outside the college to take a break and drink tea together. I learned this masala chai recipe years ago from a tea stall holder in Delhi.

300ml (1/2 pint) water
1 thick slice of fresh root ginger, peeled and squashed
2 green cardamom pods
2 cloves
2 teaspoons granulated sugar
1 tablespoon loose-leaf tea or 2 tea bags
5 tablespoons milk

Combine the measured water, ginger, cardamom pods and cloves in a saucepan and bring to a boil. Add the sugar and tea, reduce the heat to low and cook for 2 minutes, until the mixture darkens to a deep, strong colour.

Stir the milk into the pan and return the mixture to a boil, then reduce the heat and simmer for 2–4 minutes, until well infused.

Pass the masala chai through a sieve into 2 cups and serve immediately.

CHUTNEYS

AND

MASALAS

TOMATO AND DATE CHUTNEY

I was given this recipe by my friend **Sujana**, who lives in Kolkata, where this tasty chutney is served with street food snacks. The combination of sweet dates with sour tomatoes and chilli is beautiful. The mixture of spice seeds used in this recipe is known as panch phoron, a spice blend that is used abundantly in Kolkata. *See* photograph, pages 222–223.

1 tablespoon sunflower oil
1/2 teaspoon fennel seeds
1/2 teaspoon black mustard seeds
1/2 teaspoon cumin seeds
1/2 teaspoon nigella seeds (kalonji)
1/2 teaspoon fenugreek seeds
5 tomatoes, roughly chopped
1 small green chilli, finely chopped
50g (1³⁄₄oz) dates, roughly chopped
100ml (3¹⁄₂fl oz) water
1/2 teaspoon salt
1/2 teaspoon ground black pepper

Heat the oil in a saucepan over medium heat. Add the spice seeds and cook for 1 minute, until fragrant, then add the chopped tomatoes and chilli and cook for a further 5 minutes, until the tomatoes begin to soften.

Stir the dates and measured water into the saucepan, then add the salt and black pepper.

Cover the pan with a lid and cook over low heat for 30 minutes, until the mixture is thick and pulpy.

Give the chutney a good mix, then leave to cool. Serve cold. This chutney will keep in an airtight container in the refrigerator for 4–5 days.

TAMARIND CHUTNEY

You'll find tamarind chutney in most Indian kitchens. It can be made in many ways. This version is particularly sour with just a bit of sweetness, to give just the right balance for chaat. It tastes great in all the chaat recipes in this book (see pages 24, 48, 110, 156, 173 and 184), or enjoy it as a dip with snacks and canapés. *See* photograph, pages 222–223.

100g (3¹⁄₂oz) tamarind pulp
100g (3¹⁄₂oz) jaggery
5 dates, pitted and chopped
300ml (¹⁄₂ pint) water
1/4 teaspoon salt
1/4 teaspoon chilli powder
1/4 teaspoon ground cumin

Mix the tamarind, jaggery, dates and measured water in a pan and bring the mixture to a boil. Simmer for 7–8 minutes, until all the jaggery has melted and the pulp has softened.

Pass the mixture through a sieve into a bowl, ensuring you press on the residue in the sieve to extract all the tasty juices.

Heat the mixture in a clean pan over low heat for about 1–2 minutes. Add the salt, chilli powder and cumin and mix well. Take the pan off the heat and leave to cool before serving. This chutney will keep in an airtight container in the refrigerator for 15–20 days.

COCONUT CHUTNEY

This super-simple chutney completes the classic meal of Dosa (*see* page 26) and Sambhar (*see* page 33). One of the staples of Chennai cuisine, it is eaten with many different snacks and meals, including vada, idli, samosas and more. It is also great alongside dal and rice. You'll find a variation of this chutney in every household, and below is mine. *See* photograph, pages 222–223.

2 tablespoons split chickpeas (chana dal)
150g (5½oz) fresh coconut, chopped
2 green chillies, roughly chopped
2.5cm (1 inch) piece of fresh root ginger, peeled and roughly chopped
10 curry leaves
2–3 tablespoons water
1 tablespoon sunflower oil
1 teaspoon mustard seeds

Heat a dry frying pan over medium heat. Add the split chickpeas and toast for 3–4 minutes, until they are lightly browned.

Using a blender, combine the coconut, chilli, ginger and 6 curry leaves. Add the toasted chickpeas and the measured water and blend to a smooth paste. Transfer the chutney to a bowl.

Heat the oil in the frying pan over medium heat. Add the mustard seeds and remaining curry leaves and, when they begin to pop, pour the flavoured oil over the chutney and mix well. This chutney will keep in an airtight container in the refrigerator for 3–4 days.

SICHUAN SAUCE

Use with caution – this sauce is super spicy! Part of the Indian-Chinese
fusion cuisine that is well loved in India today, this sauce is used in
some very popular dishes. It also makes a great dipping sauce –
if you're brave enough to face the heat. *See* photograph, pages 222–223.

10–15 dried red chillies
100ml (3¹/₂fl oz) sunflower oil
40 garlic cloves, finely chopped
7.5cm (3 inch) piece of fresh
    root ginger, peeled and
    finely chopped
6 spring onions, finely chopped
1 tablespoon sugar
¹/₂ teaspoon table salt
1 teaspoon white wine vinegar
50ml (2fl oz) water

Cover the chillies with boiling
water and leave to soak for
15 minutes. Once they are
soft, drain off the water and
transfer the chillies to a small
food processor. Blitz to a paste,
adding just enough water to
loosen to the right consistency.
Set aside.

Heat the oil in a saucepan.
Add the chopped garlic
and cook over low heat for
10 minutes. Stir in the ginger
and cook for 5 minutes. Add
the spring onions and cook
for 5 minutes more, until the
spring onion has softened.

Stir in the chilli paste and
cook over a low heat for
10 minutes. Lastly, add the
sugar, salt, vinegar and
measured water and cook for
1 minute more. Leave to cool
and serve cold. This sauce will
keep in an airtight container in
the refrigerator for 7–10 days.

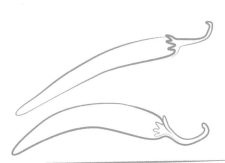

TOMATO CHUTNEY

Sour, spicy and slightly sweet, this easy chutney ticks all the boxes.
It's brilliant with snacks and finger food but also great with parathas,
rice, or as part of a thali. I like to make up a batch regularly and store
it in the refrigerator for a few days, so that we always have some
ready whenever we need to snack. *See* photograph, pages 222–223.

8 tomatoes, roughly chopped
8 garlic cloves, chopped
4 small green chillies, chopped
2 tablespoons sunflower oil
1/2 teaspoon salt
1 teaspoon granulated sugar

Using a food processor, blend the tomatoes, garlic and chillies to make a smooth paste.

Heat the oil in a saucepan and add the tomato mixture with the salt and sugar. Bring the mixture to a boil, then simmer over medium-low heat for 10–12 minutes, until the chutney thickens a little and the tomatoes are cooked. Leave to cool before serving. This chutney will keep in an airtight container in the refrigerator for 4–5 days.

PEANUT CHUTNEY

This bold, fiery chutney is simple to make and has few ingredients, but
it is deceptively complex with its many levels of flavour. It's great with
almost any snack or meal. *See* photograph, pages 222–223.

5 dried red chillies
10 garlic cloves
75g (2 1/2oz) roasted peanuts
1/2 teaspoon salt
1 teaspoon granulated sugar
1 tablespoon olive oil
4 tablespoons water

Soak the chillies and garlic cloves in a small bowl of water for 15 minutes. Drain the ingredients once the soaking time has elapsed.

Using a blender or a small food processor, grind the chillies and garlic with the remaining ingredients – the absorbed water will help to give the chutney a smooth texture. Transfer to a bowl to serve, or store in an airtight container in the refrigerator for 6–7 days.

CORIANDER AND SPINACH CHUTNEY

The addition of chana dal makes this coriander chutney completely
different to those you normally find in Indian restaurants – it has a
creamier texture and a deliciously nutty flavour. In India it's used in
all sorts of dishes, from sandwiches to bhel puri, and also makes
a great accompaniment to hot snacks such as samosa, pakora
and kachori. *See* photograph, page 227.

25g (1oz) split chickpeas
  (chana dal)
50g (1¾oz) coriander leaves
50g (1¾oz) spinach leaves
15g (½oz) mint leaves
4 garlic cloves
2.5cm (1 inch) piece of fresh
  root ginger, peeled
2 green chillies, sliced
½ teaspoon salt
50ml (2oz) natural yogurt

Heat a dry frying pan over medium heat. Add the split chickpeas and toast for 3–4 minutes, until they turn golden in colour. Tip the toasted chickpeas into a small bowl and leave to cool.

Using a small food processor, blend the coriander, spinach, mint, garlic, ginger, chillies, salt and roasted chickpeas until smooth. Add the yogurt and blend again. Transfer to a bowl to serve, or store in an airtight container in the refrigerator for 4–5 days.

MINT CHUTNEY

This is such an easy chutney to make, yet it adds so much flavour
and joy to food. I got this recipe from a street vendor in Mumbai,
who made what I considered to be the best chaat. Whenever a recipe
calls for mint chutney, this is a good version to use, and it makes
a great accompaniment to many snacks. *See* photograph, page 227.

50g (1¾oz) mint leaves
50g (1¾oz) coriander leaves
1 small onion, roughly chopped
3 small green chillies
4 garlic cloves
1 teaspoon salt
1 teaspoon granulated sugar
4 tablespoons lemon juice

Combine all the ingredients in a blender or the bowl of a food processor and process the mixture until smooth. Transfer to a serving bowl, or keep in an airtight container in the refrigerator for 4–5 days.

CURRY LEAF CHUTNEY

This exciting chutney makes use of one of the most fragrant leaves
you can cook with. I find the combination of flavours truly amazing.
I first tried it in Chennai and absolutely loved it. It works
beautifully with hot fried snacks such as vada, samosa and pakora.
See photograph, page 227.

1 tablespoon sunflower oil
2.5cm (1 inch) piece of fresh
root ginger, peeled and
roughly chopped
2 small green chillies, roughly
chopped
2 tablespoons split chickpeas
(chana dal)
50 curry leaves
1 teaspoon tamarind paste
50g (1¾oz) fresh coriander leaves
½ teaspoon salt

Heat the oil in a saucepan over medium heat. Add the ginger, chillies and split chickpeas and cook for 1 minute, until the mixture changes in colour. Add the curry leaves and fry for 2 minutes, until the leaves have softened. Stir in the tamarind paste, ensuring you mix it in well.

Tip the contents of the pan into a blender or a small food processor. Add the coriander and salt and blend the mixture to a paste. This chutney can be stored in an airtight container in the refrigerator for 4–5 days.

CHILLI AND GARLIC CHUTNEY

This is one of my favourite chutneys. Despite the fact that there are few
ingredients, it is packed full of flavour and is somewhat on the spicy
side. It makes a delicious accompaniment to any street food.

5 red chillies
15 garlic cloves
1 teaspoon salt
1 teaspoon granulated sugar
1 tablespoon coriander seeds
1 tablespoon cumin seeds
1 tablespoon vegetable oil

Soak the chillies in water for 10–15 minutes, until soft.

Drain the soaked chillies and put them into the bowl of a food processor along with the remaining ingredients, except the oil. Blend the mixture to a smooth paste.

Heat the oil in a small saucepan over low heat. Add the paste and cook for 10 minutes, until the garlic is cooked. This chutney can be stored in an airtight container in the refrigerator for 4–5 days.

CHAAT MASALA

As far as I'm concerned, this is one spice blend that should be in the cupboard at all times! Sour, refreshing and with a very tangy kick, it's the masala that makes chaat so special, but is also great added to curries, salads, chutneys and even fresh fruits.

2 tablespoons cumin seeds
1 tablespoon fennel seeds
¼ teaspoon ground black pepper
¼ teaspoon asafoetida
¼ teaspoon ground ginger
1 tablespoon black salt
2 tablespoons mango powder
  (amchur)

Heat a dry frying pan over medium to low heat. Add the cumin and fennel seeds and toast for about 2 minutes, until they start to change colour. Transfer the toasted seeds to a spice grinder and process them to a fine powder.

Put the remaining ingredients into a clean, dry jar, add the ground toasted seeds and mix well. Store in a cool, dark place. Use within 6 months.

SAMBHAR MASALA

Sambhar (*see* page 33), a staple of South Indian cuisine, can be
addictive, and this blend will help you make a really good Sambhar.
It is also a great example of how lentils can be used as spices.

50g (1³/₄oz) coriander seeds
10 dried red chillies
1 tablespoon cumin seeds
1 tablespoon black mustard seeds
1 tablespoon split black lentils
  (urad dal)
1 tablespoon split chickpeas
  (chana dal)
1 tablespoon split pigeon peas
  (toor dal)
10 dried curry leaves
1 tablespoon ground turmeric
1 teaspoon asafoetida

Heat a dry frying pan over medium to low heat. Add the coriander seeds and toast for about 1 minute, until they start to change colour. Tip the toasted seeds into a bowl, then add the red chillies to the frying pan and toast for 1 minute, until fragrant. Add the toasted chillies to the coriander seeds in the bowl.

Next, add the cumin and mustard seeds to the same frying pan and toast for 1 minute, until they begin to change colour. Add these to the chillies and coriander seeds in the bowl.

Put the dals into the frying pan and toast for 1 minute, until they begin to change colour. Once again, add them to the bowl with the toasted spices.

Combine these toasted ingredients with the curry leaves, ground turmeric and asafoetida, then use a spice grinder to process the mixture to a fine powder. Leave the spice mix to cool. Transfer the spice blend to a clean, dry jar and store in a cool, dark place. Use within 6 months.

PAV BHAJI MASALA

This spice blend is the key to producing great **Pav Bhaji**
(*see* page 130) of distinct flavour. It combines some of the basic
spices used in Indian cookery, but it's the specific quantities
of these spices that make it so different to other masalas.
Try it in other dishes using lentils and meat, too.

2 tablespoons coriander seeds
1 tablespoon fennel seeds
2 teaspoons cumin seeds
1/2 teaspoon black peppercorns
4 dried red chillies
seeds from 4 green cardamom pods
2 cloves
1 cinnamon stick
1 whole mace
1 teaspoon ground turmeric
1 teaspoon mango powder
   (amchur)

Heat a dry frying pan over low heat. Add the coriander, fennel and cumin seeds along with the peppercorns, chillies, cardamom seeds, cloves, cinnamon and mace and toast for a few minutes, stirring occasionally, until the spices begin to change colour.

Take the frying pan off the heat. Stir in the turmeric and mango powder, mix well and leave to cool.

Transfer the mixture to a spice grinder and process the mixture to a fine powder. Transfer the spice blend to a clean, dry jar and store in a cool, dark place. Use within 6 months.

DABELI MASALA

This spice blend is the key ingredient in **Dabeli** (*see* page 127).
Kept in a jar in a cool, dry place, it can be used anytime over the course
of a few months, during which time you will be able to make dabeli
in just minutes. This masala is also great used in simple potato or
vegetable curries.

2 tablespoons coriander seeds
1 tablespoon fennel seeds
1 tablespoon cumin seeds
6 cloves
4 dried red chillies
1 cinnamon stick
2 tablespoons sesame seeds
1 tablespoon Kashmiri chilli
   powder

Heat a dry frying pan over low heat. Add all the ingredients except the chilli powder and toast for a few minutes, stirring occasionally, until they just begin to change colour. Tip the mixture into a bowl to cool.

Add the Kashmiri chilli powder, then transfer the mixture to a spice grinder and process to a fine powder. Transfer the spice blend to a clean, dry jar and store in a cool, dark place. Use within 6 months.

GLOSSARY

UK	US
Aubergine	Eggplant
Beetroot	Beet
Canteen	Cafeteria
Caster sugar	Superfine sugar
Chickpeas	Garbanzo beans
Chilli/chillies	Chili/chilies
Clingfilm	Plastic wrap
Cocktail stick	Toothpick
Coriander	Cilantro
Cornflour	Cornstarch
Double cream	Heavy cream
Large egg (UK)	Extra-large egg (USA)
Filo pastry	Phyllo dough
Frying pan	Skillet
Green pepper	Green bell pepper
Heavy-based saucepan	Heavy saucepan
Hob	Stove
Icing sugar	Confectioners' sugar
Kitchen paper	Paper towels
Minced chicken	Ground chicken
Natural yogurt	Plain yogurt
Peanut	Groundnut
Plain flour	All-purpose flour
Prawns	Shrimp
Red pepper	Red bell pepper
Roasting tin	Roasting pan
Scatter	Sprinkle
Sieve	Strainer
Spring onion	Scallion
Swiss roll	Jellyroll
Tea towel	Dish towel
Tomato purée	Tomato paste

INDEX

A

almonds
  carrot halwa 206
  falooda 157
  shahi tukda 212
alu bhate 74
aubergines
  aubergine curry 101
  baigan bhaja 69

B

baigan bhaja 69
beans
  misal pav 123
  moong bean special 133
  sprouted dal chaat 173
  vegetable Manchurian 155
beetroot
  vegetable toast sandwich 120
bhakarwadi 164
bhatura 185
  chole 187
bhel 126
bread pakora 191
bream
  fish fry 78

C

cabbage
  vegetable Manchurian 155
cardamom
  cardamom and pistachio kulfi 203
  chole 187
  egg curry 98
  jalebi 197
  mango lassi 214
  masala chai 217
  pantaras 72
  pav bhaji masala 233
carrots
  carrot halwa 206
  chicken stew 87
  vegetable chow mein 119
cashew nuts
  carrot halwa 206
  kaju kishmish ice cream 210

malai prawn curry 105
moong dal with cashews 66
sweet pongal 54
upma 42
cauliflower
  cauliflower pakora 38
  pav bhaji 130
chaas 204
chaat masala 230
  bhel 126
  chicken kathi roll 89
  corn chaat 24
  cornflake chaat 48
  egg kathi roll 88
  masala chana chaat 184
  masala papads 174
  papdi chaat 110
  ragda pattice 170
chana dal vada 43
chana dal with luchi 63
chicken
  chicken chop 79
  chicken fried rice 149
  chicken kathi roll 89
  chicken lollipops 95
  chicken stew 87
  hot and spicy chilli chicken 112
  pantaras 72
  Sichuan chicken 150
  sticky Bombay chicken 134
chickpeas
  chana dal vada 43
  chana dal with luchi 63
  chole 187
  coconut boli 47
  curry leaf chutney 229
  masala chana chaat 184
  masala dosa filling 27
  potato, paneer and chickpea curry 60
  ragda pattice 170
  rice and dal papdi 40
  sambhar 33
chilli
  alu bhate 74
  baigan bhaja 69
  corn chaat 24

corn on the cob with lime and chilli 146
onion samosas 16
tawa paneer 195
chillies
  chilli and garlic chutney 229
  chilli paneer 21
  dabeli masala 233
  dabeli masala 233
  dahi vada 192
  dal chilla 92
  egg kathi roll 88
  egg rice 142
  fish fry 78
  hot and spicy chilli chicken 112
  lemon rice 52
  masala dosa filling 27
  mint chutney 228
  onion and tomato uttapam 31
  pav bhaji masala 233
  pav bhaji masala 233
  peanut chutney 225
  poha 140
  sambhar masala 232
  Sichuan sauce 224
  tamarind stuffed chillies 18
  tomato and date chutney 221
  tomato chutney 225
  vegetable Manchurian 155
chocolate toasted sandwich 160
chole 187
coconut
  bhakarwadi 164
  chana dal with luchi 63
  chicken stew 87
  coconut boli 47
  coconut chutney 220
  egg curry 98
  malai prawn curry 105
cod
  fish chop 81
coriander
  coriander and spinach chutney 228

corn chaat 24
fish fry 78
mint chutney 228
moong dal vada 39
pani puri 181
stuffed alu tikki 180
corn chaat 24
corn on the cob with lime and chilli 146
cornflake chaat 48
cream
  kaju kishmish ice cream 210
  malpua 196
  tawa paneer 195
cream cheese
  chocolate toasted sandwich 160
cucumber
  masala papads 174
  vegetable toast sandwich 120
curries
  aubergine curry 101
  chole 187
  egg curry 98
  malai prawn curry 105
  potato, paneer and chickpea curry 60
  puri alu 143
  simple fish curry 100
curry leaves
  curry leaf chutney 229
  masala dosa filling 27
  medu vada 35
  moong bean special 133
  rice and dal papdi 40
  sambhar 33
  sambhar masala 232
  vada pav 115

D

dabeli 127
  dabeli masala 233
dahi vada 192
dal chilla 92
dates
  tamarind chutney 220
  tomato and date chutney 221

dosa
  masala dosa filling 27
  plain dosa 26

E

eggs
  chicken chop 79
  chicken fried rice 149
  egg chops 84
  egg curry 98
  egg kathi roll 88
  egg rice 142
  fish chop 81
  hot and spicy chilli
    chicken 112
  kaju kishmish ice cream
    210
  omelette pav 114
  pantaras 72

F

falooda 157
fennel seeds
  bhakarwadi 164
  cauliflower pakora 38
  chaat masala 230
  dabeli masala 233
  malai prawn curry 105
  malpua 196
  pav bhaji masala 233
  tomato and date
    chutney 221
filo pastry
  onion samosas 16
fish
  fish chop 81
  fish fry 78
  simple fish curry 100
flatbreads
  bhatura 185
  chicken kathi roll 89
  egg kathi roll 88
fritters
  jalebi 197

G

garlic
  aubergine curry 101
  chicken stew 87
  chilli and garlic
    chutney 229
  chole 187

fish fry 78
mint chutney 228
misal pav 123
moong bean special 133
peanut chutney 225
Sichuan sauce 224
tomato chutney 225
ghee
  jalebi 197
  moong dal with
    cashews 66
  shahi tukda 212
  sweet pongal 54
ginger
  bhakarwadi 164
  chaas 204
  chana dal vada 43
  chicken chop 79
  chicken fried rice 149
  coconut chutney 220
  curry leaf chutney 229
  dahi vada 192
  egg chops 84
  masala chai 217
  medu vada 35
  moong dal vada 39
  Sichuan chicken 150
  Sichuan sauce 224
  sticky Bombay chicken
    134
  upma 42
  vegetable Manchurian
    155

H

halibut
  simple fish curry 100
hot and spicy chilli
  chicken 112

I

ice cream
  falooda 157
  jalebi 197
  kaju kishmish ice cream
    210
  malpua 196

J

jaggery
  coconut boli 47
  sweet pongal 54

tamarind chutney 220
jalebi 197

K

kachori
  soft kachori 62
kaju kishmish ice cream
  210
kulfi
  cardamom and
    pistachio kulfi 203

L

lemon
  lemon rice 52
  nimbu paani 163
lentils
  coriander and spinach
    chutney 228
  dahi vada 192
  dal chilla 92
  masala dosa filling 27
  medu vada 35
  moong dal vada 39
  moong dal with
    cashews 66
  mussori dal 75
  plain dosa 26
  sambhar masala 232
  soft kachori 62
  stuffed alu tikki 180
  sweet pongal 54
lime
  corn chaat 24
  corn on the cob with
    lime and chilli 146
  cornflake chaat 48
  dabeli 127
  nimbu paani 163
luchi
  chana dal with luchi 63

M

malai prawn curry 105
malpua 196
Manchurian chaat 156
mango lassi 214
masala chai 217
masala chana chaat 184
masala dosa filling 27
masala papads 174
medu vada 35

milk
  cardamom and
    pistachio kulfi 203
  carrot halwa 206
  falooda 157
  kaju kishmish ice cream
    210
  malpua 196
  mango lassi 214
  phirni 200
  shahi tukda 212
mint chutney 228
  papdi chaat 110
misal pav 123
moong bean special 133
moong dal vada 39
moong dal with
  cashews 66
mussori dal 75

N

nimbu paani 163
noodles
  Manchurian chaat 156
  vegetable chow mein
    119

O

omelette pav 114
onions
  alu bhate 74
  chana dal vada 43
  chicken fried rice 149
  chicken kathi roll 89
  chicken stew 87
  chole 187
  dal chilla 92
  egg kathi roll 88
  fish chop 81
  hot and spicy chilli
    chicken 112
  Manchurian chaat 156
  masala dosa filling 27
  onion and tomato
    uttapam 31
  onion samosas 16
  paneer-stuffed paratha
    177
  Sichuan chicken 150
  vegetable chow mein
    119
  vegetable pulao 137

P

pakora
baigan bhaja 69
bread pakora 191
cauliflower pakora 38
pancakes
dal chilla 92
malpua 196
pantaras 72
paneer
chilli paneer 21
paneer-stuffed paratha
177
potato, paneer and
chickpea curry 60
tawa paneer 195
pani puri 181
pantaras 72
papad
masala papads 174
papdi
bhel 126
papdi chaat 110
rice and dal papdi 40
paratha
paneer-stuffed paratha
177
pea-stuffed paratha 176
pav
misal pav 123
omelette pav 114
pav bhaji 130
pav bhaji masala 233
vada pav 115
peanuts
bhel 126
cornflake chaat 48
dabeli 127
peanut chutney 225
poha 140
upma 42
peas
pea-stuffed paratha 176
potato and pea samosas
190
peppers
hot and spicy chilli
chicken 112
pantaras 72
pav bhaji 130
Sichuan chicken 150
upma 42

vegetable chow mein
119
vegetable pulao 137
phirni 200
pigeon peas
mussori dal 75
sambhar 33
sambhar masala 232
pistachio nuts
cardamom and
pistachio kulfi 203
falooda 157
phirni 200
shahi tukda 212
plain dosa 26
poha 140
pomegranate
dabeli 127
potatoes
alu bhate 74
bread pakora 191
chicken chop 79
dabeli 127
egg chops 84
masala dosa filling 27
pani puri 181
papdi chaat 110
pav bhaji 130
potato and pea samosas
190
potato, paneer and
chickpea curry 60
puri alu 143
ragda pattice 170
sprouted dal chaat 173
stuffed alu tikki 180
vada pav 115
vegetable toast
sandwich 120
prawns
malai prawn curry 105
puri alu 143

R

raisins
kaju kishmish ice cream
210
sweet pongal 54
rice
bhel 126
chicken fried rice 149
egg rice 142

lemon rice 52
phirni 200
plain dosa 26
poha 140
sweet pongal 54
vegetable pulao 137
rice flour
rice and dal papdi 40
rose syrup
falooda 157

S

sambhar 33
sambhar masala 232
samosas
onion samosas 16
potato and pea samosas
190
semolina
pani puri 181
soft kachori 62
upma 42
sesame seeds
bhakarwadi 164
sticky Bombay chicken
134
shahi tukda 212
Sichuan chicken 150
Sichuan sauce 224
simple fish curry 100
soft kachori 62
spinach
coriander and spinach
chutney 228
sprouted dal chaat 173
sticky Bombay chicken
134
stuffed alu tikki 180
sweet pongal 54
sweetcorn
corn chaat 24
corn on the cob with
lime and chilli 146

T

tamarind
pani puri 181
tamarind stuffed
chillies 18
tamarind chutney 220
papdi chaat 110
tawa paneer 195

tea
masala chai 217
tomatoes
chole 187
egg curry 98
egg rice 142
masala papads 174
misal pav 123
omelette pav 114
onion and tomato
uttapam 31
pav bhaji 130
potato, paneer and
chickpea curry 60
puri alu 143
sprouted dal chaat 173
tomato and date
chutney 221
tomato chutney 225
vegetable pulao 137

U

upma 42
uttapam
onion and tomato
uttapam 31

V

vada
chana dal vada 43
dahi vada 192
medu vada 35
moong dal vada 39
vada pav 115
vegetable chow mein 119
vegetable Manchurian 155
Manchurian chaat 156
vegetable pulao 137
vegetable toast sandwich
120

Y

yogurt
aubergine curry 101
bhatura 185
chaas 204
dahi vada 192
mango lassi 214
papdi chaat 110
poha 140
simple fish curry 100
tawa paneer 195

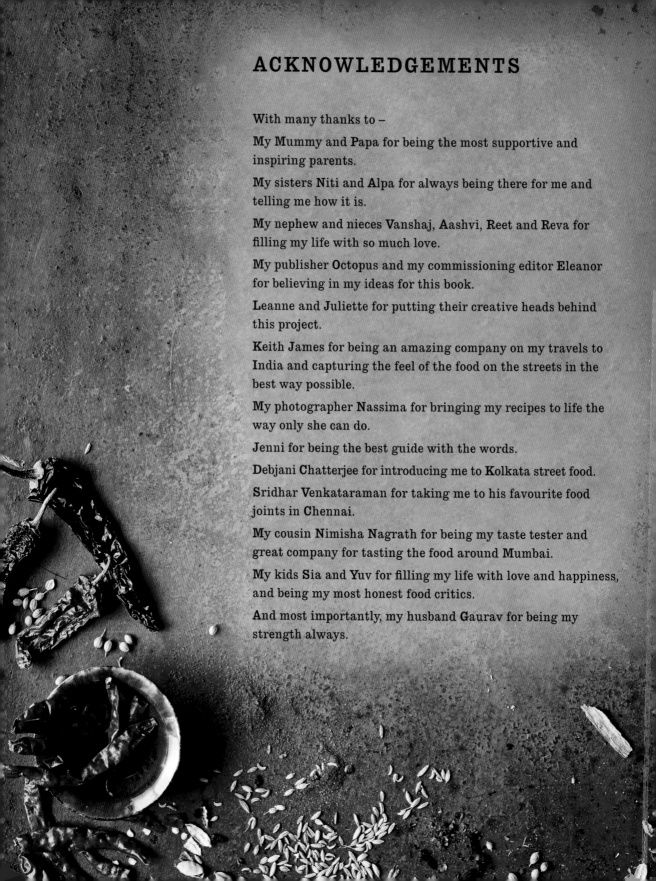

ACKNOWLEDGEMENTS

With many thanks to –

My Mummy and Papa for being the most supportive and inspiring parents.

My sisters Niti and Alpa for always being there for me and telling me how it is.

My nephew and nieces Vanshaj, Aashvi, Reet and Reva for filling my life with so much love.

My publisher Octopus and my commissioning editor Eleanor for believing in my ideas for this book.

Leanne and Juliette for putting their creative heads behind this project.

Keith James for being an amazing company on my travels to India and capturing the feel of the food on the streets in the best way possible.

My photographer Nassima for bringing my recipes to life the way only she can do.

Jenni for being the best guide with the words.

Debjani Chatterjee for introducing me to Kolkata street food.

Sridhar Venkataraman for taking me to his favourite food joints in Chennai.

My cousin Nimisha Nagrath for being my taste tester and great company for tasting the food around Mumbai.

My kids Sia and Yuv for filling my life with love and happiness, and being my most honest food critics.

And most importantly, my husband Gaurav for being my strength always.